ADHD

IT HAPPENED TO ME

Series Editor: Arlene Hirschfelder

Books in the It Happened to Me series are designed for inquisitive teens digging for answers about social issues, certain illnesses, or lifestyle interests. These books feature up-to-date information, relatable teen views, and thoughtful suggestions to help you figure out stuff. Besides special boxes that highlight singular facts, each book is enhanced with the latest reading lists, websites, and other recommendations.

The following titles may also be of interest:

ADHD

THE ULTIMATE TEEN GUIDE

JOHN ASPROMONTE

IT HAPPENED TO ME, NO. 58

Published by Rowman & Littlefield
An imprint of The Rowman & Littlefield Publishing Group, Inc.
4501 Forbes Boulevard, Suite 200, Lanham, Maryland 20706
www.rowman.com

Unit A, Whitacre Mews, 26-34 Stannary Street, London SE11 4AB

British Library Cataloguing in Publication Information Available

Library of Congress Cataloging-in-Publication Data

Names: Aspromonte, John, 1977– author.
Title: ADHD : the ultimate teen guide / John Aspromonte.
Description: Lanham : Rowman & Littlefield, [2019] | Series: It happened to
  me ; no. 58 | Includes bibliographical references and index.
Identifiers: LCCN 2018024321 (print) | LCCN 2018037501 (ebook) | ISBN
  9781538100394 (electronic) | ISBN 9781538100387 (cloth : alk. paper)
Subjects: LCSH: Attention-deficit disorder in adolescence. |
  Attention-deficit disorder in adolescence—Social aspects. |
  Attention-deficit disorder in adolescence—Treatment. | Teenagers—Life
  skills guides.
Classification: LCC RJ506.H9 (ebook) | LCC RJ506.H9 A87 2019 (print) | DDC
  616.85/8900835—dc23
LC record available at https://lccn.loc.gov/2018024321

∞™ The paper used in this publication meets the minimum requirements of American National Standard for Information Sciences—Permanence of Paper for Printed Library Materials, ANSI/NISO Z39.48-1992.

Printed in the United States of America

To everyone who struggles with,
or knows someone who struggles with,
ADHD.
With knowledge, persistence, and a sense of humor,
you can find the key to your success.

Contents

Acknowledgments

I would like to acknowledge my wife, Bernadett, who is not only the author of chapter 4 but also the coauthor of my life. Her valuable insights, knowledge, and guidance were an integral part of this book.

I would also like to acknowledge my son, John. I am so proud to be your dad.

To Mom and Jerry, your support is immeasurable.

I would also like to acknowledge the many educators, researchers, and clinicians who have helped me forge my path over the years.

Introduction

When I mention the term *attention-deficit/hyperactivity disorder*, what comes to mind? Maybe you think of someone who is always zoning out or someone with boundless energy, or maybe you think of someone who always says what's on his or her mind. Maybe that term makes you think of a person who has a great sense of humor or is very creative. Perhaps you don't even think you know anyone with ADHD. There is a good chance that the term *ADHD* means different things to different people. Within ADHD is a collection of behaviors that we all may have experienced at one time or another, either in ourselves or in someone else. Did you know that up to 5 percent of schoolchildren in the United States have ADHD? That is a lot of people. As a student, this means that there is a good chance someone in your class has ADHD, maybe even you. ADHD has become a commonly referred-to disorder and a household name, but many people still have questions about what exactly ADHD is and how it can affect us.

True or false: ADHD is a simple problem of being hyperactive and not listening when someone is talking to you. False! ADHD is a complex disorder that involves impairments in focus, organization, motivation, emotion, memory, and other functions of the brain's management system. In addition, ADHD can affect schoolwork, social life, family life, and the way you feel about things. Learning the facts about ADHD and busting many of the common myths that people believe are important if you want to understand and live with ADHD successfully.

The purpose of this book is to provide the definition of and information about ADHD and its effect on school, family, and social life. This book is for anyone who wants to learn factual information about ADHD and also hear about the difficulties and successes of other young people who have ADHD. Along the way we will explore what students like you think about ADHD and learn where to go to find information and communities of people who are dedicated to the study of it.

WHAT IS ADHD?

What is attention-deficit/hyperactivity disorder, or ADHD? Defining each of the terms in ADHD will help us to have a better understanding of what it is. *Hyperactivity* can be defined as moving around a lot. This is easy to see with our eyes; it makes a person look fidgety and restless. Hyperactivity may be one of the first things that we notice about someone with ADHD. Having a disorder means that you have a problem that causes a lack of functioning in an area of your life, in this case because of problems caused by a lack of attention and hyperactivity.

Attention deficit is a lack of attention, but what is attention and how do you tell when there is a lack of it? If you think about it, we use the word *attention* all the time but can you define it? You may use words like *notice, understand,* or *comprehend.* Is it looking, hearing, feeling? What does it mean to attend to something? How do we focus our attention? What does it look like when our attention is not focused? We have all experienced a situation where someone is looking at us, but we still wonder if they are paying attention to us. Is attention deliberate? In other words, do we need to do it on purpose like reading a book, or can it be passive, something that we can do without any effort like watching a movie or listening to music? Maybe there is no attention, merely perception. When we tell someone to pay attention, we are really telling him or her to look, listen, and understand what we are doing. But we can attend without looking, or hearing, or even understanding.

Attention is not an easy thing to define. Imagine you are at a Broadway show. All of the lights are turned down and there is a spotlight on the stage. Attention is kind of like the spotlight; in a play, it's the lighting designer's way of telling us what to *pay attention* to at the moment. There may still be other things in the theater that are visible or audible to you, but the spotlight is what you *should be* focusing on, that is, if you want to know what is going on in the show. What would this show be like if there were no spotlight, but you had background music, people talking, and the show playing all at the same time? It would be much harder to focus on the place where that spotlight used to be or to even know what to look at.

What is an attention deficit—a lack of attention? How do we measure a lack of attention? Can it be tested on a point system? Is it measured in inches, or feet, or maybe in degrees like a thermometer? Who exactly defines when we do not have quite enough attention? These are hard questions, and there are no perfect answers for them.

There is no single test that can definitively tell us if we have an attention deficit. So how do we know? We may not have a perfect way to measure attention; however what we do know is that there are consequences of not paying attention. Consequences such as missing information, not following directions, forgetting or losing things. These consequences of a lack of attention are much easier to measure and can help determine if you have problems with attention. In this chapter we will define what attention-deficit/hyperactivity disorder is, look at three aspects of ADHD, and answer some common questions about ADHD.

Important Statistics on ADHD

According to the US Centers for Disease Control and the *Diagnostic and Statistical Manual*, fifth edition (*DSM-5*), approximately 5 percent of children in the United States have ADHD.[1] This is known as the prevalence of ADHD. As of 2011 approximately 6.5 million children had been diagnosed with ADHD in the United States. Interestingly, the number of people diagnosed with ADHD has gone up every year since 2003. This rise in the number of diagnoses is known as the incidence.[2]

The percentage of children diagnosed with ADHD has increased in recent years from 7.8 percent in 2003 to 9.5 percent in 2007 to 11 percent in 2007. Rates of ADHD diagnosis have increased by 3 percent per year from 1997 to 2006 and 5 percent a year from 2003 to 2011. Boys were more likely to be diagnosed with ADHD than girls—with boys at 13.2 percent and girls at 5.6 percent—and the average age of diagnosis was seven years old.[3]

How is it possible for the number of people with ADHD to rise every year, and what does it mean? Does this mean that more and more children are getting ADHD, and is the rate really rising in our country? The best way to answer questions like these is to look at national data. ADHD is not uniformly spread across the country. For example, some states have much higher incidence and prevalence of ADHD and some have lower. If we look internationally some countries have higher rates of ADHD and some have lower.

This rise in the number of cases of ADHD can be attributed to a number of factors, including diagnostic criteria changing, an increased demand on children in general, or a legitimate rise in ADHD rates.

If we think about the diagnostic criteria described earlier in the chapter—inattentiveness, hyperactivity, and impulsivity—what would happen if the diagnostic criteria of ADHD changed? Changing the criteria can affect the number of individuals who have an illness. For example, since there is no test for ADHD

Did you know that there are more people with ADHD in the United States than the populations of New York City, Los Angeles, and Philadelphia combined? © *iStock / Melpomenem*

the medical community agrees on a collection of symptoms; over the years as the medical and psychological community gains more and more understanding of a group of symptoms, the criteria can change. This is kind of like a school changing the passing grade on a test. If the passing grade is a 60, one hundred kids may pass, but if the passing grade is 70 only eighty kids may pass. Likewise, since there is no test for ADHD, people must agree on what the *cutoff line* is for symptoms, and as this line moves it can affect the number of people that meet the criteria and are diagnosed in a year.

Another factor that can affect the prevalence is increasing demands on students and school systems. As the education system demands more and more from students, the bar is raised year after year. What was considered average academic performance thirty years ago is no longer considered average; the demands have gone up. A recent article in the *Journal of the American Medical Association* outlined this trend:

- From 1981 to 1997, the average weekly homework for first through third graders more than doubled, and parents spent 30 percent more time teaching their preschool-age children letters and numbers.

- In 1998, only 30 percent of teachers thought it was necessary to teach a child to read in kindergarten; by 2010, that figure had shot up to over 80 percent.
- Preschool-age children who were enrolled in full-day academic programs ballooned from 17 percent in 1970 to nearly 60 percent by the 2000s. At the same time, ADHD diagnoses were steadily rising. Between 2003 and 2011 alone, the percent of students between the ages of four and seventeen who had been diagnosed with ADHD jumped from 7.8 to more than 11.[4]

These increased demands can make it seem like some children who may have been functioning in the average range a number of years ago are now unable to handle academic demands. These rising standards may be a factor in the increasing number of students who are referred for evaluation or have trouble in school. It is important to note that academic achievement standards vary from state to state, as do the number of ADHD diagnoses. Jeffrey Brosco, who was the lead researcher on a University of Miami study, said that "from time spent studying to enrollment rates in pre-primary programs, everything had increased. And not surprisingly, in the past 40 years we also saw ADHD diagnoses double."[5]

The Symptoms of ADHD

ADHD is classified as a neurodevelopmental disorder.[6] This means that ADHD is a difference in the way the brain develops. ADHD and the brain will be discussed further in chapter 4; however, there are three main symptoms of ADHD, and in order to be diagnosed with the disorder, you have to have either some or all of these symptoms:

1. Inattention
2. Hyperactivity
3. Impulsivity

Inattention is when we have trouble focusing our attention or become distracted easily. Some people who are diagnosed with ADHD are primarily inattentive. This means that they mostly have the symptom of inattentiveness and not hyperactivity and impulsivity. Inattentiveness can have an impact on a person's daily functioning. For example, if you have trouble paying attention, it makes it hard to read a book; take notes in a class; organize, plan, and follow through on longer school projects; and many other tasks. If you have trouble paying attention you may miss details when doing work and make what others may call careless errors. Following and remembering long instructions may be difficult if you miss some of the instructions.

"In class, I had a kind of lag time, 'cause in-between me figuring out what had been going on, the entire class moved on, so I missed out on information. So that was one of the biggest things—missing out—taking a longer time to get the entire idea."[a]

To some, a person who is inattentive may appear to be losing interest or zoning out. It can look like the person is not interested in what is going on or is even being rude. Without being able to plan and organize, a person who is inattentive may do things sloppily, her belongings may be disorganized or messy, and she may lose things or appear forgetful. When tasks become difficult or never get accomplished, a person may start to avoid those tasks altogether because he knows that he will not be able to complete them. Avoiding tasks may make a person appear lazy, but this is not the case; people with ADHD are not lazy.

The next symptom of ADHD is *hyperactivity*. Hyperactivity is when you have trouble sitting still. When you are in a situation that requires you to sit still, like school, it can feel like you have ants in your pants or you may feel fidgety or restless. When you are outside the classroom you may look and feel like you are constantly in motion and being driven by a motor. Things like waiting in line or staying seated at the dinner table can be really difficult. What can end up happening is that a person with ADHD leaves his seat when he is not supposed to. To some this may look like misbehavior or not following the rules, but it is not; it is just very difficult for someone who is hyperactive to be still for long periods.

Impulsivity is when you do not think things through before doing them. Impulsivity often goes hand in hand with hyperactivity. When certain situations require

Three Types of ADHD

1. *Combined presentation*: a person has symptoms of inattention, hyperactivity, and impulsivity
2. *Predominantly inattentive presentation*: a person mostly has symptoms of inattention
3. *Predominantly hyperactive-impulsive presentation*: a person mostly has symptoms of hyperactivity and impulsivity[b]

"My parents did provide support . . . with homework; making sure I was on top of things. It kind of got to the point where it was nagging, but that's how they got the actual answer from me. They had to play 20 questions. I wasn't trying to withhold information; it just took 20 questions to get the full description. You couldn't ask, 'What do you have for homework?' It was like, 'Do you have any homework?' 'Yes.' 'What is it?' 'Math.' 'What's it on?' 'This stuff.' 'Do you have English homework?' 'Yes.' . . . They had to go through a much larger spectrum of questions just to get the answer to, 'Do you have any homework?' Otherwise they wouldn't know what it was that needed to be done. And they wouldn't know whether or not I was done so 'you can go watch TV,' or 'you can go play.' That was incredibly helpful."
—a college student with ADHD remembering doing homework as a child[c]

a person to think out a response or wait her turn in conversation or sit for extended periods of time, a person with ADHD may not be able to do those things and instead do something else. A great example of impulsivity is calling out answers in class without raising your hand. A student like this may think then say without thinking about the consequences of what she is going to say or looking for others' reactions. "Did I say that out loud? I wish I had a take back." Outside of the classroom, impulsivity can look like you are interrupting people when they are talking. In later chapters we will look at the consequences of impulsivity.

Executive Functions

Executive functions may sound like the name of a party that you would attend wearing a tuxedo and talking to the CEO of a major corporation, but that's not what we're talking about. These executive functions are a group of thought processes that many people with ADHD have trouble with. These thought processes include planning and goal setting, organizing, prioritizing, working memory, shifting, inhibition, and self-regulation. Think of a thought process as a procedure we do with our minds, a progression of mental steps that can get us from point A to point B. We may need thought processes like these to go grocery shopping or plan our weekend. There are seven primary executive functions:[7]

1. Planning and goal setting—ability to think through a task, make plans, set reasonable goals, and problem solve

2. Organizing—ability to put things in an order that helps in the completion of tasks
3. Prioritizing—ability to recognize which components of tasks are most important to complete and focus on the relevant details
4. Working memory—ability to hold and manipulate relevant information in memory
5. Shifting—ability to devise new strategies and be cognitively flexible when a situation changes
6. Inhibition—ability to inhibit or constrain thoughts and actions that are inappropriate for a situation
7. Self-Regulation—ability to regulate one's behavior and monitor one's thoughts and actions

A great example of a project or task that involves executive functions would be studying for end-of-the-year final exams. There are a lot of executive functions involved in planning your studying for finals. All of this planning must take place before you get to the actual studying part. If someone were to record your inner dialogue while you were planning, it might sound like this:

OK, my finals are in two weeks. I have to decide when and where I am going to do my studying [planning]. Maybe I will go to the library, but I have to find out what hours they are open [planning]. I also need to think about how many pages a day to read if I want to get all the studying done [goal setting]. I should make a list of all the chapters and divide the pages between the fourteen days [goal setting]. OK, which subject should I study first? Maybe biology; I have the lowest grade in that course and it has the most pages to read [prioritizing] but I should make a plan B in case I need a break from biology and maybe come back to it later [shifting]. I have to promise myself not to get distracted and go out and party instead of finishing my studying even if it gets difficult [inhibition]. Even if my friends are texting me or I am having trouble getting through my studying [inhibition]. Lastly, I have to be absolutely sure to go to sleep on time even if I am on a roll, because I have to get enough sleep to study again tomorrow [self-regulation], being tired tomorrow will ruin tomorrows studying.

Planning to study for finals would involve all of these executive functions in order to be successful in studying. Let's imagine for a minute that you were not able to do all of that planning and just jumped in and started reading. What could happen? You might not get to all of the reading because you did not pace yourself. Maybe you would start with a subject that did not require you to study much. You might go to the library when it is already closed, wasting time. There are many consequences to not being able to do these tasks before you begin to study. Now let's imagine doing all that planning and then not being able to concentrate while studying—ugh, so frustrating! Right?

Some, but not all, people with ADHD also have problems with executive functions. It would make good sense that someone who is inattentive, hyperactive, and impulsive would have trouble doing some of the things described earlier, but don't worry. In chapter 5 we will discuss ways to support and help you succeed in the studying process. It is debatable whether problems with executive functions can exist on their own without ADHD and to what extent. Regardless, it is noteworthy that problems with the seven primary executive functions can exist in individuals with ADHD and that accommodations can be provided.

How Do You Get ADHD?

No one knows for sure. ADHD probably stems from interactions between genes and environmental, or nongenetic, factors.[8] Studies have been done on individuals with ADHD, and it is clear that ADHD can run in families. People with family members who have ADHD have a higher percentage chance of having it themselves. For example, if you have a parent with ADHD, you have a higher chance of having it. In addition, twin studies have shown that if one twin has

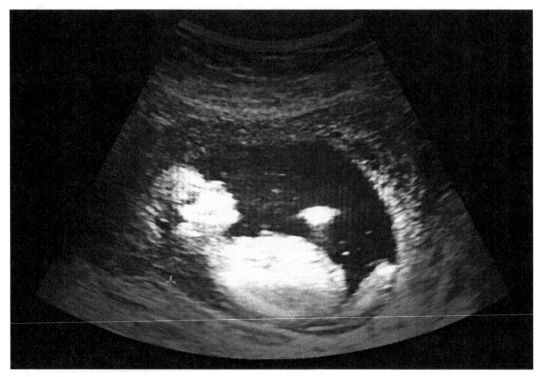

Did you know that ADHD has been linked to risk factors that can begin during your mother's pregnancy, before you are born? © *iStock / kornnphoto*

ADHD, the other has a higher chance of having it, supporting the fact that there is a genetic component.[9]

There are also risk factors for having ADHD. There is good evidence that being born with a low birth weight and being exposed to prenatal smoking and alcohol consumption are all risk factors for ADHD.[10] In other words, it is more likely that someone with ADHD was exposed to these things in the womb and at birth than someone who doesn't have the condition; there is a relationship between these risk factors and having ADHD.

Another important point is that, with few exceptions, ADHD is something that you are born with. There are known medical conditions as well as injuries to the brain that can affect attention and motor activity. These are not the same as ADHD. ADHD is a condition of its own. Similarly, diet does not cause ADHD. Although eating a healthy and balanced diet may make it easier to focus or make you feel less hyperactive, ADHD itself is independent of the diet that one eats.

Learning Disabilities

Although ADHD is not considered a learning disability, some people with ADHD can also have learning disabilities, which according to the *Diagnostic and Statistical Manual of Mental Disorders*, fifth edition (*DSM-5*), can happen as often as 50 percent of the time.[11] The *DSM-5* is a book written by doctors, including psychologists and psychiatrists and other medical professionals, that contains groups of symptoms and disorders as well as other important information. Books like this provide a general consensus or agreement by the medical and psychological community of the symptoms of a disorder.

Depending where you look—education law, psychological and psychiatric diagnosis, or commonly used phrases—there are different ways of defining learning disabilities. According to the Individuals with Disability Education Act of 2004, which is federal law that ensures educational services to children with disabilities, the term *specific learning disability* means "a disorder in one or more of the basic psychological processes involved in understanding or in using language, spoken or written, which disorder may manifest itself in the imperfect ability to listen, think, speak, read, write, spell, or do mathematical calculations."[12] The *DSM-5* refers to learning disabilities as *specific learning disorders*[13] and classifies them into categories such as specific learning disorder with impairment in mathematics, writing, or reading. In addition, frequently people may know some of these types of learning disabilities with their more common names such as dyslexia, which means a disability in reading or comprehending words; dyscalculia, which means difficulty with number sense, memorization of arithmetic facts, or accurate or fluent calculation; or dysgraphia, which is a disorder of writing.

It is important to note that a *specific learning disability* does not simply mean that you are "bad at math" or "not a great reader." It means that you have a problem with a basic psychological process that manifests itself in the disability. Only someone trained to measure psychological processes can determine the root cause of a learning disability. To do so one would need an evaluation, which will be discussed in chapter 3.

Although it is possible for someone to have both ADHD and a learning disability, it is not always the case. According to the *DSM-5*, up to 50 percent of children with ADHD also have a co-occurring learning disability.[14] For these students it is like a double whammy: problems with attention as well as a specific learning disability. School can be a real challenge for these students, and they may require special help in school. Special supports in school will be discussed in chapter 5.

Behavioral Problems

Having ADHD does not automatically mean that you have behavioral problems. However, up to 40 percent of children with ADHD also meet the criteria for oppositional defiant disorder (ODD). Oppositional defiant disorder is defined in the *DSM-5* and can look like this: losing your temper, not following directions, annoying others, and arguing. ADHD researcher Russell Barkley states that a large part of ODD is the inability to manage emotions. Because of the inability to inhibit responses and be emotionally impulsive, ADHD can be diagnosed as ODD. In addition he states that treatment for ADHD often leads to a reduction in the symptoms of ODD as well.[15]

Giftedness

Having ADHD or a learning disability does not mean that you have a low level of intelligence or that you are not talented. The term *gifted* is defined by the federal law in the No Child Left Behind Act of 2002 as "students, children, or youth who give evidence of high achievement capability in areas such as intellectual, creative, artistic, or leadership capacity, or in specific academic fields, and who need services and activities not ordinarily provided by the school in order to fully develop those capabilities."[16] It is important to note that having a high level of intelligence or being gifted does not mean that school is easy for you. You must also be in the right environment. Education is all about the right fit. We can think about the analogy of having the right tool for the job or an appropriate vehicle for the road we were driving on. It would be no easier to maneuver a Formula One race car in a parking garage than it would be to drive a hybrid on a race track. Although both are great cars, if we put them in the wrong environment, the cars will not perform very well. Education is like this: if we put a learner in the wrong environment, no matter what his gifts, it will do him no good.

There are many examples of high-achieving people who are both gifted and have learning disabilities or ADHD. It is possible for a student to be what we call twice exceptional. These are students who may have ADHD and/or a specific learning disability as well as being identified as gifted or talented in one or more areas. It is important for a school to understand the specific needs of students identified as twice gifted because these students have the qualities and struggles of children with ADHD and a specific learning disability as well as the qualities and struggles of gifted individuals.[17] As we will see in chapter 6, social and emotional difficulties can result from having learning disabilities or ADHD. Social and emotional difficulties can also stem from being gifted. It is important to understand the consequences so they can be addressed.

Gifted students often possess the following traits:

Intelligence—high level of intelligence
Motivation—strong desire to learn
Interests—unusual or advanced interests
Communication skills—high level of communication skills verbally, with numbers, symbols, or art
Problem-solving ability—effective and creative problem-solving ability
Memory—large capacity to remember things
Curiosity—tendency to be inquisitive and interested in exploring
Reasoning—high level of reasoning abilities
Imagination/creativity—often very creative
Humor—good sense of humor[18]

In addition to having both a learning disability and ADHD, a student may also be gifted or talented, although being gifted or talented does not necessarily mean that school is easy.

That was a lot of information, right? Well, even with all the information that you just read, you may still be left with more questions about ADHD. What follows is a Q&A section about ADHD. If you have even more questions, the "Resources" section will help you find answers.

Questions and Answers about ADHD

What Is a Diagnosis, and How Do You Get Diagnosed?

A diagnosis is when a doctor looks at a person and determines what is wrong by considering the collection of symptoms she has. With ADHD a doctor would look for symptoms of inattention, hyperactivity, and impulsivity. When we use the term *diagnosis*, we are usually referring to the fact that you have been evaluated by a doctor or multiple doctors and they agree that you meet the criteria (have symptoms like the ones outlined in the *DSM-5*) for ADHD. Being diagnosed usually means that you have been evaluated by a psychologist, who usually has a PhD and performs psychological testing, and also by a psychiatrist or another medical doctor. Doctors do testing and ask questions that are meant to help them understand whether you meet the criteria for ADHD. A doctor may ask your teachers or family questions about you; she may also perform some psychological tests that are meant to figure out if you have ADHD symptoms. It is important to go to a knowledgeable professional because he will try to determine whether the symptoms of ADHD are due to ADHD or something else. For example, many of the symptoms of ADHD like inattention and hyperactivity are also symptoms of being tired or not getting enough sleep or being stressed out. A doctor can figure out if your symptoms are due to ADHD or to something else.

How Do I Get an ADHD Diagnosis? Is There a Test for ADHD?

There is no single test for ADHD and getting a diagnosis of ADHD varies from state to state. According to the Centers for Disease Control most children under the age of six who are diagnosed with ADHD are diagnosed by a psychiatrist. Most children who are diagnosed over the age of six are diagnosed by a psychologist. These doctors will generally ask questions, perform tests, and make a decision if you meet the criteria for ADHD.

Wait, I Feel Like That Sometimes—Do I Have ADHD?

It is important to realize that the symptoms that are listed at the beginning of the chapter happen to everyone. Haven't you ever felt like it was hard to pay attention or like you couldn't sit still or like you spoke too soon and should have thought a minute before you answered? The answer to many of these questions is probably yes. It is important to understand that all of these things are quite normal and happen all of the time. Maybe you were hungry and didn't eat lunch, or you did not get enough sleep the night before, or you were stressed out about midterms or finals and it caused you to experience some of these symptoms. All of these examples can cause us to be inattentive or impulsive. The difference between instances like these and having ADHD is that if you have ADHD, you don't need any of these circumstances to experience the symptoms; they happen all on their own. The other difference is that the symptoms have to persist for more than six months and usually have to begin before the age of twelve to receive a diagnosis of ADHD.

If I Have ADHD Does That Mean I Am Stupid?

Absolutely not! Many people with ADHD are very bright. Having ADHD means that you have inattention, hyperactivity, or impulsivity to a degree that it interferes with your daily functioning. It does not mean that you are unintelligent.

If I Have ADHD, Does That Mean Something Is Wrong with Me?

Again, absolutely not. ADHD involves abnormal (unusual) brain development. Does that mean it is bad? It is not good or bad, but different. There are lots of people with abnormal brain development. Having a genius-level IQ like Albert Einstein or Steven Hawking is also not normal. Terms like *abnormal* or *unusual* mean just that—something is out of the ordinary. As we will see in later chapters there are things that individuals with ADHD are better at doing than others; we call these the ADHD superpowers. Whenever someone is different it can cause difficulties fitting into what is normally expected, and what may be normal for some may not be normal for you. Abnormalities or differences can come with advantages and disadvantages. It is important to recognize both of them.

Is ADHD a Learning Disability?

ADHD is not classified as a learning disability. Even though it is not classified as a learning disability, it can still cause problems learning. If we think back to the beginning of the chapter and the effect that inattention, hyperactivity, and impulsivity can have on someone trying to learn, those effects can be cumulative. This means that the constant missing of information and the inability to do long-term assignments and homework can cause a student to fall behind in knowledge and also skills. If not treated year by year the falling behind can cause more serious problems in school. What started as an inability to pay attention can turn into problems missing information and practicing skills, and after a number of years can result in problems that appear as a lack of skills. This can make it appear that someone with ADHD has a problem learning instead of problems paying attention.

Does ADHD Go Away? Can I Be Cured or Do I Grow out of It?

Some research—for example, research by Dr. Harold Kopliwicz from the Child Mind Institute—states that people who are diagnosed with ADHD in childhood grow out of the disorder, but this may not be totally true. Many times what happens is that individuals grow out of some of the hyperactive symptoms such as restlessness and being fidgety. This can make it appear that they have grown out of ADHD. What may be happening is that some of the symptoms of hyperactivity decrease because the brain develops more in the areas that control motor movement. At the same time, what also appears to be happening is that the individuals do not grow out of the inattentive symptoms of ADHD as they get older.[19] Hyperactive and impulsive symptoms oftentimes get the most attention from others. When those symptoms go away what is left are the inattentive symptoms of ADHD. They may go unnoticed leading some to believe that ADHD has been outgrown.

Do People with ADHD Really Have Trouble Paying Attention?

The term *focusing attention* is important because it may be helpful to look at ADHD not as a problem that involves paying attention. People with ADHD are often paying attention, to everything, at the same time! The problem that they really have is focusing attention on a single task.

Hopefully after reading this chapter you have a better understanding of the symptoms, related problems, and some important statistics on ADHD. In the following chapters we will continue to explore many different aspects of ADHD and hear experiences from other young people with ADHD.

THE HISTORY OF ADHD

A diagnosis is a collection of symptoms, behaviors, or patterns that doctors and scientists agree on. Throughout history people have had inattention, hyperactivity, and impulsivity, but attention-deficit/hyperactivity disorder did not get its name until 1987. That year the *Diagnostic and Statistical Manual*, third edition, was revised and released.[1] Before 1987 ADHD was known as *attention deficit disorder* (no hyperactivity in the name). Before 1980 it was known as *hyperkinetic reaction of childhood*. Before 1968 it was known as *minimal brain dysfunction* and prior to that *minimal brain damage*. It is important to realize that ADHD has changed over the years and so has our definition.

One way to think about this is if we compare ADHD to a country whose name and borders have changed over the years. Did you know that before Alaska was a US state it was owned by Russia? It was purchased by the United States in 1867 and became a state in 1959.[2] Although Alaska was part of a different country, the natural inhabitants of Alaska still remain the same. Maybe the borders have changed a little but the central core is the same and many still speak the same language. ADHD is similar. Its name and some of the behaviors that define it have changed, but the core symptoms have stayed the same. Some people may think that because the name ADHD did not exist thirty years ago, there was no such thing as ADHD. This would be like saying that there was no such thing as cancer or diabetes before the name existed in medical books. As our understanding of science gets better, so does our understanding of ADHD.

Why has the name changed so much over the years? Since the first descriptions of ADHD in medical writings appeared over three hundred years ago, our understanding of science has changed a lot. Hundreds of years ago scientists did not even have microscopes or any of the modern equipment or understanding that we do today. In the beginning when there was little understanding of the brain, the focus was mostly on what we could see, behavior. Although observations of behavior were useful, without modern scientific knowledge it was hard to understand why people with ADHD behaved as they did, and what to do about it. Reasons such as bad parenting or lack of morality were often used to describe bad behavior. Much like the time when scientists thought the world was flat or the sun was the center of the universe, an increased understanding of science proved that these beliefs were not true.

Scientific understanding can have an impact on the way we see the world. For example, before the 1850s there was no germ theory. This meant that it was not known exactly what caused colds or infections, because bacteria and viruses had not been discovered. It was not understood why people got sick, which led to many made-up theories, including smelling rotting material or breathing in other bad smells. In fact the term *malaria* means "bad air." Now we know that mosquitos carrying a parasite are the main cause of malaria. In some religions, sickness was seen as a punishment for immoral actions, and to some sickness was due to individual weakness that could be changed by an increase in education or moral values.[3] As science discovered that bacteria, viruses, or parasites caused illness, there was a change in the way sickness was viewed socially. As it became clear that people were not the cause of their own illness, it also became clear that individuals were not to blame. Similarly, as we have gained a better understanding of ADHD, we now know that it is not caused by bad parenting, lack of morality, or bad choices. We do not blame individuals with ADHD for their differences and do not have to view their differences in a negative way.

In the following pages we will look at the history of ADHD from its first reference in 1775 until the present day. Keep in mind that we will use the term *ADHD* even though that exact phrase did not appear until it was first published in 1987.

The Eighteenth and Nineteenth Centuries

Melchior Adam Weikard (1742–1803)

Melchoir Adam Weikard was a German-born physician who first published a medical textbook in 1775 titled, *Der Philosophische Arzt*, or *The Philosophical Physician*, which describes symptoms very similar to what we now think of as ADHD. This is believed to be the earliest known reference to ADHD in the scientific literature. Sir Alexander Crichton was previously thought to be the first to publish on ADHD in 1798. However, the *Der Philosophische Arzt* contained a chapter on attention deficits called "Attentio Volubilis," or "Attention Is Turning." In this chapter Weikard describes many of the symptoms that we currently associate with ADHD, such as inattention and distractibility. Wiekard stated, "Those, who have a lack of attention, are generally characterized as unwary, careless, to describe." He also stated that "Every humming fly, every shadow, every sound, the memory of old stories will draw him off his task to other imaginations."[4] Weikard's observations are important in the history of ADHD because he appears to be the first person to describe these symptoms in scientific literature. It is noteworthy that although Wiekard seems to be the first to describe ADHD, he also had a number of false beliefs or claims about ADHD that have been since proven false by over 240 years of science. Some of these beliefs noted that ADHD occurred more in boys than in girls, that ADHD was caused by bad parenting, and even that it occurred more in certain nationalities—all of which we know is not true.

Alexander Crichton (1763–1856)

Sir Alexander Crichton was a Scottish physician who described some of the symptoms of what we now call ADHD. Crichton described the symptoms of inattention and hyperactivity in the book chapter "On Attention and Its Diseases" published in a medical textbook in 1798. The topic of attention was something that interested Crichton; he called it the *parent of all our knowledge*.[5] This means that before we can think, do, or learn about anything, we must first be paying attention to it. Attention must always come before learning, much like parents must precede their children. Crichton believed inattention could be something a person was born with. Further he stated that the wavering of attention was natural and could be due to an injury, being bored, or eating a large meal. Crichton also believed that the amount of attention you had for something could be the result of how much something interested you. It is a common belief today that those with ADHD pay attention better when things interest them. Crichton did not believe that attention was voluntary. He thought that when you chose to pay attention to something else, it was because that other thing was simply more interesting. Many of Crichton's observations are consistent with what we now know about ADHD, making him an important figure in its history.

Heinrich Hoffman (1809–1894)

In 1848 German physician Heinrich Hoffman published a children's book called *Struwwelpeter*, or *Shock-Headed Peter*, which described a boy who did not wash his hair, cut his fingernails, or bathe. The story was part of a collection of short stories meant to teach children lessons in manners and good behavior. Hoffman was a medical doctor and had studied attention. Within his book was "The Story of Fidgety Philip." "The Story of Fidgety Philip" is one of the first documented stories of a child with the hyperactive symptoms of ADHD. In the story, a boy

A German postage stamp depicting Harry who looks in the air, a character from the Heinrich Hoffmann book *Struwwelpeter.*© *iStock / clu*

that had trouble sitting still would rock back and forth in his chair at the dinner table until at one point he fell over, taking the whole dinner table with him, angering his parents. In addition to fidgety Philip, *Struwwelpeter* contained another story called "Harry Who Looks in the Air." This story appears to describe a child with poor attention who after not looking where he was walking falls into a river and loses his school notebook.

The Story of Fidgety Philip

"Let me see if Philip can

Be a little gentleman;

Let me see if he is able

To sit still for once at table":

Thus Papa bade Phil behave;

And Mamma looked very grave.

But fidgety Phil,

He won't sit still;

He wriggles,

And giggles,

And then, I declare,

Swings backwards and forwards,

And tilts up his chair,

Just like any rocking horse—

"Philip! I am getting cross!"

See the naughty, restless child

Growing still more rude and wild,

Till his chair falls over quite.

Philip screams with all his might,

Catches at the cloth, but then

That makes matters worse again.

Down upon the ground they fall,

Glasses, plates, knives, forks, and all.

How Mamma did fret and frown,

When she saw them tumbling down!

And Papa made such a face!

Philip is in sad disgrace.

Where is Philip, where is he?

Fairly covered up you see!

Cloth and all are lying on him;

He has pulled down all upon him.

> What a terrible to-do!
>
> Dishes, glasses, snapt in two!
>
> Here a knife, and there a fork!
>
> Philip, this is cruel work.
>
> Table all so bare, and ah!
>
> Poor Papa, and poor Mamma
>
> Look quite cross, and wonder how
>
> They shall have their dinner now.[a]

Charles Darwin (1809–1882)

I know what you may be thinking. Why is Charles Darwin included in our discussion of ADHD? After Darwin published *The Origin of Species* laying out the theory of natural selection and the basis for evolution, the way people viewed science changed. Darwin believed the species that could best adapt to the environment were the fittest and would survive. Darwin's theories had a huge impact on how people viewed biology. They also had a huge impact on how people practiced science. Darwin had an impact on observation, classification, and data collection. Although Darwin did not study ADHD there is no doubt that his impact on the world of science affected those who would come after him who did study ADHD.

Sir George Frederick Still (1868–1941)

Often the symptoms of ADHD, especially impulsivity and hyperactivity, make it appear as if a person is not following the rules. School is a good example of this. Maybe a student is told to sit but gets out of his seat without asking, or instead of raising her hand, a student calls out the answer. When someone does not follow the rules, it is easy to label this as *bad behavior*; however, for someone with ADHD it may just be impulsivity. In 1902 Sir George Frederick Still, an English pediatrician, described children who had a *moral defect* that resulted in them not following the rules.[6] It is important to recognize that Still believed not following rules was due to poor moral choices by children with problems sustaining attention. This is where scientific understanding can change our social understanding of behavior. If we were to believe that a student called out without raising his hand because of a *poor moral choice*, we may have a very different opinion about the behavior than if we believe he called out due to impulsivity. If we believe that a child made a poor moral choice, we would be more prone to blame the student for her behavior, whereas if she called out due to impulsivity we would be more understanding.

It appears that in the beginning of modern-day psychology and psychiatry, different doctors focused on different aspects of ADHD: Crichton, the inattention; Hoffman, the hyperactivity; and Still, the impulsiveness and lack of understanding of consequences. All of these symptoms would eventually become what we now call ADHD. It is important to note that these descriptions are rather negative. Most of them focus on behaviors that were seen as troublesome or not the norm. To understand the experiences of those with ADHD, it is helpful to understand how the views of ADHD have changed over the years. One has to look no further than these descriptions, because they do not describe any of the positive traits that people with ADHD exhibit. As science moved into the twentieth century, discoveries were made at an amazing pace. We began to have a better understanding of disease, genetics, medications, and psychology. This led to new descriptions and reasons for why people acted as they did and also new understanding of how to treat them. ADHD was no different.

The Twentieth Century

Franklin Ebaugh (1895–1972)

In 1923 psychiatrist Franklin Ebaugh found evidence that symptoms of ADHD could arise from brain injury caused by encephalitis lethargica.[7] Encephalitis is an inflammation of the brain that is usually caused by infection or virus. During 1917–1928 there was an encephalitis lethargica epidemic, which means that millions of people all over the world had the disease. In the children who survived, encephalitis lethargica created symptoms that were very similar to ADHD, including lack of attention, hyperactivity, and difficulty behaving in school. Remember from chapter 1 that there are different reasons for people having the same behavior. In the case of encephalitis lethargica, children were thought to have damaged brains from the illness. Franklin Ebaugh conducted a study on children who had encephalitis and found that they did in fact have some of the same symptoms. This led to the belief that ADHD could be caused by brain damage and eventually gave rise to the first name of ADHD, minimal brain damage.

Franz Kramer (1878–1967) and Hans Pollnow (1902–1943)

As science entered the twentieth century, German psychiatrists Franz Kramer and Hans Pollnow described ADHD-like symptoms in a condition they called hyperkinetic disease of infancy.[8] Hyperkinetic disease of infancy was focused on hyperactivity. They described a pattern of hyperactivity that, unlike other disorders, did not happen while the person was asleep. The fact that the hyperactivity did not happen in the patient's sleep and was not caused by encephalitis led them to believe that *this* hyperactivity was different from that experienced by patients with disorders like encephalitis. Kramer and Pollnow did not see a connection between their patients and those who had encephalitis and therefore did not think that hyperactivity was due to brain damage.

Charles Bradley (1902–1979)

In the 1930s Charles Bradley was the first to treat hyperactivity with Benzedrine.[9] Benzedrine is a stimulant that was used to treat the hyperactive and inattentive symptoms in children with brain injuries as well as those with behavioral problems. The medication was observed to help the behavioral symptoms in children with emotional disturbances and it also improved school performance. This success paved the way to other medications that were used to treat the symptoms of ADHD.

Leandro Panizzon (1907–2003)

In 1944 Italian chemist Leandro Panizzon first synthesized the chemical compound methylphenidate in the lab. Methylphenidate was marketed under the name Ritalin in 1954.[10] Methylphenidate is another example of a stimulant that is used to treat the attention and hyperactivity symptoms in ADHD. It is still considered to be one of the leading medications used to treat ADHD symptoms. Panizzon named his newly discovered compound after his wife Marguirita, or Rita, naming the compound Rita-lin.

ADHD Name Changes: 1950s to the 1980s

Minimal Brain Damage and Minimal Brain Dysfunction (1950s)

In the 1950s, the name for the group of symptoms that would later be called ADHD was minimal brain damage, partially due to the fact that some scientists had seen a connection between children who had encephalitis and children who had ADHD. In addition some scientists tried to determine the main differences in people who had brain damage and those who did not. Some of the key differences observed were attention and hyperactivity, leading some to believe that problems with attention and

THE HISTORY OF ADHD **23**

**National Institute of Mental Health Funds Study
on Stimulants (1967)**

In 1967 the National Institute of Mental Health funded research on the
effect of stimulants on children with hyperactivity.[b] With the success of other
stimulants in decreasing the symptoms of ADHD and also a better understanding of medications, the government funded research into the effects of stimulants on ADHD. The results of those studies confirmed that stimulants were effective for the treatment of ADHD.

hyperactivity were due to brain damage.[11] However as data accumulated showing
that many children with these problems did not have brain damage or encephalitis,
the name was eventually changed to minimal brain dysfunction. It is important to
distinguish between the terms *damage* and *dysfunction*: *damage* implies the brain has
been altered or injured in some way, whereas *dysfunction* implies the brain is somehow not functioning properly or doing the normal job.

Hyperkinetic Reaction of Childhood (1968)

The second edition of the *Diagnostic and Statistical Manual of Mental Disorders*
included a definition for hyperkinetic reaction of childhood, which eventually
became ADHD. This definition characterized children who were overactive,
restless, and distractible; had short attention spans; and stated that the behaviors
usually diminished by adulthood.

Attention Deficit Disorder: With and
Without Hyperactivity (1980)

In 1980 the *Diagnostic and Statistical Manual of Mental Disorders*, third edition
(*DSM-III*) changed the definition of hyperkinetic reaction of childhood to what
is now a little more familiar, attention deficit disorder (ADD). ADD was seen as
an overarching diagnosis that had two different subtypes, those with hyperactivity
and those without.

Attention-Deficit/Hyperactivity Disorder (1987)

In 1987, the *DSM* revised its definition of ADD.[12] In this version of the *DSM*, ADHD was considered one condition. In addition to the change in name, ADHD was becoming more accepted in society. As you will read in the next chapter about the history of education, in 1990 the government issued a memo stating that ADHD could be a reason to receive education or disability services in school. Many individuals received diagnoses of ADHD during this time. During this time there was also a large increase in the number of people who were prescribed medication for ADHD. The consumption of stimulant medication rose from about two million people to sixteen million between 1991 and 1999.[13]

Summary

In the last 240 years since Melchior Adam Weikard published his work on disorders of the brain, much has been written on the subject of ADHD. It has been viewed as a moral disorder, a result of brain damage, a nervous system disorder, a dysfunctional brain, and now a neurodevelopmental disorder. It is important to realize that the way people view ADHD has changed over the years not only as a product of our better understanding of science but also as a product of the environment and the demands that are now placed on children.

For example, think about what goes into a diagnosis of ADHD today in terms of poor academic functioning, such as doing poorly on tests, not completing assignments, or not being able to sit still for six to eight hours a day in school. Many of these requirements did not even exist hundreds of years ago. It is no wonder that many scientists first focused on behavior and not learning. Two hundred and forty years ago many children did not go to school or spent minimal time there. This is a trend that persisted until the twentieth century. Would those children have been diagnosed with ADHD today? We will never know. Now up to 11 percent of children in school have the diagnosis of ADHD.[14] A disability can be a product of our environment. In order to have a disability you must have the inability to do something. This inability must in some way affect your daily life. This is important to think about because as we will see in chapter 3 there are requirements to receive special education services, and part of those requirements is that you need special education due to a disability.

In addition to the changes in name, ADHD has become more accepted in society. As you will read in the next chapter about the history of education, in 1990 the government issued a memo stating that ADHD could be a reason to receive education or disability services in school. Many individuals received diagnoses of ADHD during this time, and there was also a large increase in the number of people who were prescribed medication for ADHD. Between 1991 and 1999, the consumption of stimulant medication rose from about two million people to sixteen million.[15]

If we think about the incidence of ADHD rising every year since 2003, we may want to consider the effects that the environment has on what we think of as a disorder or disability. If we look at how the demands placed on students in the last few hundred years have increased, it makes sense that with increased demands there would be more students having difficulty meeting those demands.

Questions and Answers

Do I Have Brain Damage If I Have ADHD?

No, ADHD is considered a neurodevelopmental disorder. This means that somewhere in your brain's development, usually before you enter grammar school, there is a slower development in the areas of your brain that control your ability to pay attention and remain still. This is different than brain damage, which is caused by some kind of physical injury. Unlike what scientists thought many years ago, ADHD is not caused by injury to the brain. It is not brain damage.

Is ADHD a Made-Up Disorder?

No. ADHD is a name for a collection of symptoms that include inattention and hyperactivity. Over the years our understanding of why these symptoms happen has changed and so has the name science has chosen to call it. ADHD is the most recent name for these symptoms that have been around for many years. Much like other illnesses that did not have names before science could understand them, neither did ADHD. This does not mean that it did not exist or that it is *made up*.

ADHD is also something that is not visible with your eyes. Unlike a physical trait like having brown hair or blue eyes, you cannot exactly see ADHD. What you can see are the behaviors that have been described in earlier chapters. Sometimes when people cannot see something or fully understand it, they are led to think it does not exist.

What Was School Like for Someone with ADHD Two Hundred Years Ago?

You may be asking yourself if it was easier or harder to have ADHD a long time ago. Schools have changed a lot in the last few hundred years. In 1919 in the

United States, there were almost two hundred thousand one-room schoolhouses. These were small buildings where all the students of different grades were in one room together with a single teacher. Usually a student brought a small slate, which was like a personal chalkboard, and some books to school. In addition students usually had to walk to school, sometimes long distances. Things like the resource

Timeline for ADHD

1775	Melchior Adam Weikard described symptoms of inattention and hyperactivity.
1798	Sir Alexander Crichton described the symptoms of inattention and hyperactivity.
1848	German physician Heinrich Hoffman described the story of fidgety Phil and Johnny head in the clouds.
1902	Sir George Frederick Still described children with a *moral defect*.
1923	Franklin Ebaugh found evidence that ADHD could arise from brain injury.
1937	Charles Bradley used Benzedrine to treat hyperactive children.
1944	Leandro Panizzon synthesized Ritalin, a stimulant to treat ADHD.
1952	The original *DSM* used the term *minimal brain dysfunction* for ADHD.
1967	The federal government funded a study of stimulants on children with hyperactivity.
1968	*DSM-II* used the term *hyperkinetic reaction of childhood* to describe ADHD.
1980	*DSM-III* used the term *attention deficit disorder: with and without hyperactivity* to describe ADHD.
1987	*DSM-III-R* used the term *attention-deficit/hyperactivity disorder* for the first time to describe ADHD.
1994	*DSM-IV* continued to use the term *attention-deficit/hyperactivity disorder* to describe ADHD.
2000	*DSM-IV-TR* continued to use the term *attention-deficit/hyperactivity disorder* to describe ADHD.
2013	*DSM-5* continued to use the term *attention-deficit/hyperactivity disorder* to describe ADHD.[c]

room and special education services did not exist. It was also acceptable in many schools for teachers to use harsh or embarrassing punishment when students did not follow the rules or do what they were told.

What Is a Stimulant, and Why Are They Used to Treat ADHD?

Stimulant is a word that is used to describe some medications that are used to treat ADHD. Stimulants can increase alertness, attention, and energy and also have other side effects such as raising blood pressure and heart rate. Since many people with ADHD may appear to have plenty of energy, it may seem funny to give them something that would stimulate them. Chapter 4 will contain more information about the brain and medications. Stimulants can help individuals with ADHD to have calm bodies and to concentrate.

SPECIAL EDUCATION LEGISLATION

··

D id you know that until 1975 the government did not have to educate students with disabilities?[1] In this chapter we will learn how that has changed over the years. Now every student in the United States has the right to a free and appropriate public education, regardless of disability, race, or ethnicity. How did this change happen? In chapter 2 you learned that over time views and opinions change. In the United States during the 1950s and 1960s views about human rights, and rights for individuals with disabilities, were changing. Equal rights became an important topic. The idea of equality eventually led to changes in the law. From then until now there have been enormous changes in the education system and education law in the United States. Education laws are the laws that govern the educational system in the United States. These laws apply to children and young adults who are in school and provide their school rights, including special education.

Laws are important to the field of special education. If we were to imagine that special education was a professional sport, laws would be the *rules* by which the game is played, and much like professional sports the rules can change. In special education laws determine how and when individuals should get special education services, as well as define your rights as a student, what types of services you should get, and how much they should cost. Even in professional sports with rules there still needs to be a referee to make sure the rules are followed and decide how the rules should be applied in particular instances. We can think of the judicial system as the *referee* that can interpret the rules and make sure that the game is played fairly.

The law can be confusing because it is complex and ever changing. Sometimes as a law gets older it is changed or amended. Much like the milk in your refrigerator, some laws have expiration dates. Unlike the milk in your refrigerator, laws can be reused after they expire in a legislative process called reauthorization or reenactment. This means there is a process of debating, changing, and then resigning an act into law. It can then reemerge with another name. This is the case with many of the laws that will be discussed in this chapter. For example, the

Public Laws

Laws are often denoted by the initials P.L. When you see a P.L. before a law it means Public Law, for example, P.L. 89-142 is the Education for All Handicapped Children Act of 1975. The numbers in the law stand for the 89th sessioin of Congress and the 142nd law that was passed during that session. The first congressional session was held in July of 1789.[a]

Elementary and Secondary Education Act of 1965 later became the No Child Left Behind Act of 2002 and most recently became the Every Student Succeeds Act of 2015. For this reason it benefits you to know the history of how the laws were created because in some instances three different names are really the same law.

What do all these laws have to do with ADHD? Under the law, ADHD can be considered a disability. This means that ADHD falls under both special education and disability law. For this reason, these laws are entwined with the history of ADHD. In this chapter you will learn about the history of education law and special education law, as well as the process of getting special education services and how that applies to ADHD.

How the Law Works

In the United States there are federal laws, state laws, and local laws. Federal laws apply to the entire United States. Federal laws are meant to provide a general rule system and are sometimes not very specific, so they are open to interpretation. States and towns can also make their own laws as long as they are consistent with federal laws.

The supreme law of the land is the United States Constitution, and it governs everything. When our founding fathers drafted the Constitution, providing education for citizens was not part of the law. This means that it was up to states and local agencies to make their own educational laws. However, now there are federal education laws and states do follow them. You may ask, "Why do states follow federal education law if they don't have to?" The answer is that if states do not follow federal education law, they are not eligible to receive federal funding, and all public schools receive some federal funding. During the 2012–2013 school year, for example, $1.15 trillion was spent on education in the United States and

Civil Rights and Disability Laws

Civil rights laws govern your rights as a human being and are your basic protections. The Bill of Rights was the outline for civil rights, including freedom of religion and the right to vote. Everyone—including people with disabilities—is covered under civil rights laws.

Disability laws protect people with disabilities. A person with ADHD is considered by law to have a disability. Any law that protects people with disabilities will also protect someone with ADHD.[b]

approximately 8 percent of this funding, or $92 billion, came from the federal government.[2] This is a reason why states and towns follow federal education law.

In addition to laws the United States has a judicial system. Courts exist at the local, state, and federal levels. Laws are written by the legislative branch of the government and signed into effect by the executive branch. After a law is passed it is interpreted by the judiciary system. When a court interprets a law, it decides how the law is carried out. The term *legal precedent* is a fancy way of saying that after one court makes a decision, other courts will follow it. This is important to recognize because as we look at the history of education law you will read about laws and court cases, both of which helped shape the history of education.

Special Education Law in the Beginning

In 1867 the US Department of Education was created by president Andrew Johnson. Its main purpose was to collect information and statistics about the nation's schools.[3] Over the course of many years the Department of Education has changed. In October 1979, Congress passed Public Law 96–88, the Department of Education Organization Act, that created our present-day Department of Education. It began operations in May 1980.[4]

In 1954 the Supreme Court made a landmark ruling in the case of *Brown v. Board of Education*. The decision stated that students could not be segregated in school based on skin color and that schools could no longer operate by the principle of *separate but equal*. This was an important court case for the education system and also for the civil rights of students in the United States. Until this ruling, some states were separating students into different schools or classrooms based on their skin color. In this case, the Supreme Court ruled that the segregated states

> **Did You Know?**
>
> The Fourteenth Amendment of the US Constitution required that states provide equal protection to everyone under the law.[c]

and schools were in violation of the Fourteenth Amendment of the Constitution. It is an example of the court declaring state laws unconstitutional. This led to the protection of civil rights of school children. It's also an example of people's changing ideas about equality leading to changes in the law.

Elementary and Secondary Education Act of 1965

The Elementary and Secondary Education Act of 1965 (ESEA) P.L. 89-10 was signed into law by president Lyndon Johnson.[5] This law was later called the 1994 Improving America's School Act, then the 2002 No Child Left Behind Act, and then the 2015 Every Student Succeeds Act. The ESEA exemplified a law that has been reauthorized many times with different names. The ESEA is important because it was the first law to give funding to disadvantaged students. Later, it was the first law to require standardized testing in schools. So if you are wondering why you have to take math and reading tests every year, it is because of this law.

This law is relevant to ADHD because it requires that you be tested in academic subjects every year. Students with ADHD may require changes to testing procedures, like an extended time or a distraction-free room. These are called accommodations. Without accommodations, tests may not be measuring how much someone really knows. For this reason, you should know your rights with regard to receiving accommodations for the tests that you take every year.

Section 504 of the Rehabilitation Act of 1973

Section 504 of the Rehabilitation Act of 1973 was designed to protect individuals with disabilities in programs and schools that receive federal funds. This is an example of a civil rights law that protects individuals with disabilities. Section 504 does not allow discrimination on the basis of disability. It states that "no otherwise qualified individual with a disability in the United States . . . shall, solely by reason of her or his disability, be excluded from the participation in, be denied the benefits of, or be subjected to discrimination under any program or activity receiving federal financial assistance."[6] This meant that schools were required to provide a free and appropriate public education to everyone, regardless of their disability. In order to qualify for Section 504 you only need to have a disability.

Just because someone has a disability does not mean he has to have poor grades or be bad at school.

Section 504 was not used very often after it was passed. Since section 504 was particularly useful for students with ADHD, the US Department of Education issued a memo in 1991 specifically addressing the classification of students with ADHD. It clarified that students with ADHD were indeed eligible for special education services in categories such as other health impairment (OHI). It also outlined Section 504 services that schools could offer students with ADHD.[7]

Education Act of 1974

The Federal Education Records Privacy Act of 1974 (FERPA) is important because it protects the privacy of your educational records and personally identifiable information.[8] This is a federal education law that applies to students in schools that receive federal funding, whether they are in special education or not. FERPA has three main purposes:

1. Protects the privacy of your educational records
2. Allows you or your parents access to your educational records
3. Gives you the ability to dispute anything in those records

Over the years there have been amendments to FERPA that have redefined the extent to which your records are private and also the extent to which you are entitled to records.

FERPA is important to students with ADHD because they should know that their evaluations, reports, classification, and academic records are private and may not be shared with anyone outside the school unless their parents (or the student himself if he is eighteen) give the school permission (called consent) to do so.

Federal Education Records Privacy Act of 1974 (FERPA)

Under FERPA an educational record is defined as "directly related to a student; and maintained by an educational agency or institution."[d] Educational records can include progress reports and disciplinary records as well as evaluations and individual education plans.

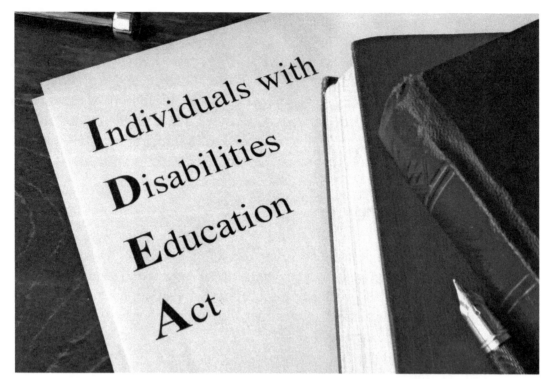

The Individuals with Disabilities Education Act started out as the Education for All Handicapped Children Act and is an example of a piece of legislation that has been reenacted and has changed names over the years. © iStock / designer491

The Education for All Handicapped Children Act of 1974 (P.L 94-142)

In 1975 Congress enacted the Education for All Handicapped Children Act (EAHCA), or P.L. 94-142. Today it's called the Individuals with Disabilities Education Act, or IDEA.[9] P.L. 94-142 was designed to ensure that all children with disabilities had access to a free and appropriate education regardless of their disability, in the least restrictive environment. This is an example of a special education law that is applicable to schools that receive federal funding.

Six core principles in IDEA have remained the same since 1975. Every student is entitled to the following:

1. Free and appropriate public education.
2. Evaluation if a disability is suspected.
3. Individualized education program (IEP) to reach educational goals.
4. Education in the least restrictive environment. *Least restrictive environment* refers to educating students with disabilities in the classroom with peers their same age to the maximum extent possible, without removing them.

5. Due process. Parents and children have rights with regard to their education setting or plan. The education plan or setting cannot be changed by the school without the parent or student knowing about it or having a way to object.
6. Parental participation. Parents must have a say in the education decisions of their children.

When the EAHCA was renamed the IDEA, its name changed to reflect *people first* language: *individuals with disabilities* instead of *disabled people*. Also, the term *handicapped* was discontinued, which many found to be offensive. Other disability categories were added to the IDEA such as traumatic brain injury and autism spectrum disorder. IDEA is the most comprehensive special education law in the United States; it covers almost all of the services and procedures in special education.

The Americans with Disabilities Act of 1990

In 1990 the Americans with Disabilities Act (ADA) was signed into law. It was a civil rights law for all people with disabilities in the United States. ADA uses the same language that Section 504 regulations use for disability and is an example of one law using the definition in another law. ADA gives individuals with disabilities civil rights protections that are like those provided to individuals on the basis of race, sex, national origin, and religion. It guarantees equal opportunity for individuals with disabilities in employment, public accommodations (curb cut outs, wheelchair ramps), transportation, state and local government services, and telecommunications.[10] ADA included state and government services such as education and schools whether those schools received federal assistance or not, public or private. The law states that priority should be given to accommodations that help people "get in the front door." ADA also has a provision for examinations and courses that allow for accommodations to be made for testing (educational or professional) that assure examinations measure what they are intended to measure, rather than reflecting the individual's impaired sensory, manual, or speaking skills.

Legal Resources on ADHD and Education Law

In the last twenty-six years the offices of the US Department of Education released a number of memorandums clarifying the law, specifically with regard to ADHD. What follows are some legal memorandums that are directly related to ADHD.

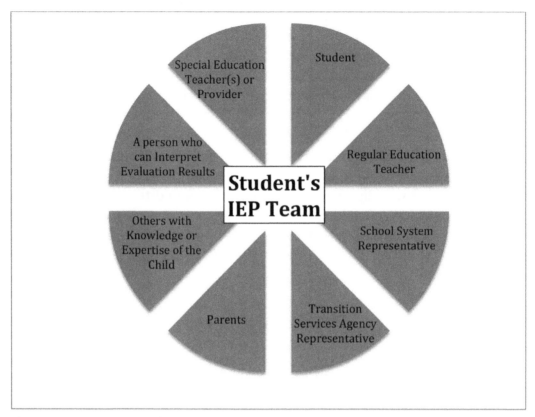

Special Education Teacher(s) or Provider

Student

A person who can Interpret Evaluation Results

Student's IEP Team

Regular Education Teacher

Others with Knowledge or Expertise of the Child

School System Representative

Parents

Transition Services Agency Representative

The IEP team consists of many individuals who are part of the educational decision-making process for a student. *Courtesy of the author*

On September 16, 1991, the US Department of Education Office of Special Education and Rehabilitative Services published a memorandum in response to the growing number of children who were diagnosed with ADHD and were not receiving educational services. It clarified that children with ADHD were covered under Section 504 as well as IDEA. It also stated that students with ADHD could be classified under other health impairment and had the right to request an evaluation if they were suspected of having ADHD.[11]

In 1992 the US Office for Civil Rights published a memorandum called "Evaluation of Children Who May Have ADHD." This 1992 memorandum clarifies that schools must evaluate children who are suspected of having ADD based on parental request. It states, "Under Section 504, if parents believe their child has a disability, whether by ADD or any other impairment, and the local education agency (LEA) has reason to believe the child needs special education or related services, the LEA *must evaluate the child* to determine whether he or she is disabled as defined by Section 504."[12]

In 2016 the US Department of Education Office for Civil Rights published a document called "Know Your Rights: Students with ADHD." This document clarifies the obligation of schools to provide equal educational opportunity to students with ADHD under Section 504 of the Rehabilitation Act of 1973.[13]

Putting It All Together: The Individualized Education Program Process

As you read in the beginning of the chapter, laws are the rule book for special education. Many of the steps you have to go through to receive special education are the result of the laws you have just read. The IEP process that is outlined in IDEA is a good example of this. As mentioned, IEP stands for individual education program and anyone who receives special education services has an IEP. There is a ten-step process to receiving an IEP. It is important to understand this process so you can be an active participant in decisions that are made about you.

Step 1: If you, your family or your school suspects that you may have a disability, you can request an evaluation. Your parents or guardians must give permission before an evaluation can be performed.

Step 2: The evaluation can be used to determine whether you are eligible for special education services. Parents have the right to dispute the outcome of the evaluation and request an independent one. During the evaluation you, your teachers, and/or your parents may be asked questions about you and your education needs. You may also be asked to take some tests, which are usually given by a school psychologist. After the evaluation a report is made about the results.

Step 3: Eligibility is decided. A group of education professionals meet, sometimes called the IEP team, to decide whether you meet the classification for a disability.

Step 4: If you are found eligible, the team of educational professionals has thirty days to meet and draft an IEP to support educational services.

Step 5: The school system schedules and conducts an IEP meeting. The school must contact the parents, schedule a meeting, and inform parents of time and place, purpose of the meeting, and who will be attending. Parents may also invite people who have knowledge of the student. Parents meet with the IEP team and discuss the educational supports and goals that will be listed in the IEP.

Step 6: The IEP is written, spelling out educational services. Parents must agree to these services before the school can give them. If parents disagree they can request mediation, make a complaint, or request a due process hearing.

Step 7: The services are provided. A copy of the plan is given to teachers and parents and service providers, and it outlines everyone's responsibilities for carrying out the plan including accommodations, modification, and supports.

Step 8: Progress toward annual goals is measured and reported to parents.

Step 9: The IEP is reviewed at least once a year by the team and the parents. It is revised and updated as needed.

Step 10: The student is reevaluated. This reevaluation is often called a triennial and is done at least every three years to determine if the student still qualifies for special education and what the services should be.[14]

Your Individualized Education Program

According to IDEA, the IEP must contain specific components:

Current performance: This can include results from your evaluation, reports from teachers, or report cards. Documents that provide an understanding of your educational performance can be summarized in the IEP.

Annual goals: IEPs must have specific goals and objectives to reach those goals. This is so that your progress can be measured throughout the year.

Special education and related services: This includes types of modifications to the educational program as well as related services such as counseling, occupational therapy, speech and language services, or physical therapy.

Participation with nondisabled children: As we read earlier in the chapter, students in special education must be placed in the least restrictive environment. The IEP must document any time that you will not be placed in a regular education classroom.

Participation in state- and district-wide tests: As we read in the No Child Left Behind Act and the Every Student Succeeds Act, all children must be tested every year. There is no exception for special education; however, there may be more flexibility in the accommodations for testing and they must be listed here in the IEP.

Dates and places: The IEP must list what the services are, how long they will be provided and when they will end.

Transition services: The IEP must state at age fourteen what transition coursework you will need and at age sixteen what transition services you will need to reach post-school goals.

Age of majority: At least one year before you reach the age of majority, you must be informed of the rights that will pass to you. For example, according to FERPA, at age eighteen the right to your records transfers to you.

Measuring progress: The IEP must state how progress will be measured and how parents will be informed of that progress.[15]

Now that you have learned about the laws as well as the IEP process, you may have more questions regarding special education. What follows are some commonly asked questions in this area.

Questions and Answers

Does Having a Disability Qualify Me for Special Education Services?

Having a disability does not guarantee you the ability to receive special education services. You must have a disability and because of the disability have a need for special education services.

How Do I Get a Diagnosis of ADHD?

You receive a diagnosis by going to a psychologist, psychiatrist, or physician and having an evaluation completed.

What Is the Difference between a Diagnosis and a Classification?

A physician or psychologist outside of the school can give you a diagnosis of ADHD. Within special education you receive a classification, not a diagnosis. Within the school system there is no classification of ADHD; however, the symptoms of ADHD may fall under the classification of other health impairment, or OHI. In order to receive a classification, you must go through the IEP process.

What Is the Difference between an IEP and a 504 Plan?

An IEP is an individual education program meant to help a student who has been classified under one of the thirteen disability classifications in IDEA. In the case of ADHD, it would fall under the OHI classification. An IEP is meant to outline services that you will receive in school as a result of your disability. A 504 plan is created because you have a disability that interferes with your ability to learn. You may receive in-class accommodations for your disability but not be placed in a special education classroom. You do not have to have poor grades to have a 504 plan.

What Is the Difference between an Accommodation and a Modification?

An accommodation is a change in the environment to somehow meet the need of a student. This accommodation allows the student to learn in the same environment and meet the same educational expectations as other students. Some examples of accommodations are verbal instructions instead of written, extended time on a test, and sitting in the front of the room during class.

Modifications are changes that alter the educational standards that a student must meet. Examples may be reducing the number of items on a test or lowering the reading level of an assignment.

Imagine that you need help to get into a building. An accommodation would be a wheelchair ramp to the entrance; a modification would be rebuilding the entrance and putting it at street level.

I Want to Learn More Stuff—Where Should I Look?

There are a lot of great resources out there. For resources regarding education law and your rights, try the US Department of Education website. This is a great resource for information regarding your rights and other topics.

In this chapter you learned about the history of special education law and how it applies to ADHD. You also learned about the IEP process including how to receive an IEP. If you would like to learn more about ADHD and education law look for the links at the end of the chapter for additional readings. In the next chapter we will change gears and learn more about the brain with regard to ADHD.

Timeline of Education Legislation and Policy in the United States

1867   Creation of the US Department of Education

1954   *Brown v. Board of Education*

        Supreme Court ruling that segregation in schools was unconstitutional.

1965   P.L. 89-10: Elementary and Secondary Education Act

        Commitment to provide federal funding to disadvantaged students

        Paved the way for children with disabilities

1965   P.L. 89-313: Elementary and Secondary Education Act Amendments

        Released federal funding for disadvantaged students

1966   P.L. 89-750: Elementary and Secondary Education Amendments

        Created federal funding opportunities for children with disabilities

1969   P.L. 91-230: Elementary and Secondary Education Amendments

Created the Education of the Handicapped Act of 1970

Created the legislative definition of a learning disability

Acknowledged the needs of gifted and talented students

1972   PL 92-424: Economic Opportunity Act

10 percent of Head Start be devoted to children with disabilities

1972   *Parc v. Commonwealth of Pennsylvania* and *Mills v. Board of Education of the District of Columbia*

Legal victories prohibiting the exclusion of students from schools because of disabilities

1973   Section 504 of the Rehabilitation Act

Protects the civil rights of individuals with disabilities in federally funded programs

School must provide a free and appropriate education to those with disabilities

1974   P.L. 93-380: Education Amendments of the Elementary and Secondary Education Act

States must educate all students with disabilities

Must use least restrictive environment

Due process procedures

Must have funding for gifted students

1974   P.L. 93-280: Education Act

Family and Education Records Privacy Act (FERPA)

Protects the privacy of educational records

Restricts access to those with a legitimate interest

Gives families rights to access the educational records of their children and request changes or corrections

1975   P.L. 94-142: Education for All Handicapped Children Act

Free and appropriate public education for children with disabilities

1982   *Board of Education of the Hendrick Hudson Central School District v. Rowley*

Court case that defined what "appropriate" education was

1983 P.L. 98-199: Education of the Handicapped Act Amendments
      Addition of transition planning from secondary school to adulthood (age
          twenty-one)
1984 P.L. 98-524: Carl D. Perkins Vocational Education Act of 1984
      Support vocational educational programs
1986 P.L. 99-372: Handicapped Children's Protection Act
      Reimbursement of attorney fees if parents get services
1986 P.L. 99-457: Education of the Handicapped Act amendments
      Mandated the establishment of education services for children three to
          five years old
1988 P.L. 100-407: The Technology-Related Assistance for Individuals with Dis-
          abilities Act of 1988; Technology Act of 1998 (P.L. 105-394) (ATA)
      Amended in 1994 (P.L.103-218) and updated
      Provided funding to develop comprehensive statewide technology-
          related assistance programs. Established the definition of "assistive
          technology" as "any item, piece of equipment, or product system . . .
          that is used to increase, maintain, or improve the functional capabili-
          ties of individuals with disabilities"
1990 P.L. 101-336: Americans with Disabilities Act of 1990
      Prohibited discrimination against individuals with disabilities
      Extended disability coverage from the public to the private sector
          whether the schools receive federal funding or not
      Covered accommodations
1990 P.L. 101-392: Carl D. Perkins Vocational and Applied Technology Educa-
          tion Act of 1990
      Equal access to vocational programs for students with disabilities
1990 P.L. 101-476: Education of the Handicapped Act Amendments
      Created the Individuals with Disabilities Education Act (IDEA)
      Used *people first* language
      Thirteen disability categories, expanded services to individuals with
          traumatic brain injuries and autism spectrum disorders
      Required the inclusion of a plan for transition services from high school
          to adult living

1991   Joint Policy Memorandum

1991   Memorandum from the U. S. Department of Education; children with ADD/ADHD may be eligible for special education services under several existing categories including specific learning disability, other health impairment, and emotional disturbance; circumstances under which schools must provide services and supports under Section 504 of the Rehabilitation Act.[17]

1992   Office of Civil Rights Memorandum

Explains the school's responsibilities to children with ADHD

1994   P.L. 103-227: Educate America Act of 1994

Funding for the development and implementation of eight broad national goals. Goals 2000: Educate America Act aimed at reforming education, to be achieved by the year 2000

1997   IDEA Amendments

Students with disabilities would be included in statewide assessments

ADHD could be included under other health impairment

A major retooling of IDEA. Modified the construction of individual education programs; enhanced the educational accountability of students with disabilities

2002   P.L. 107-110: No Child Left Behind

Represents a major effort at educational reform and increased accountability with achievement testing

2004   P.L. 108-446: IDEA

Latest reauthorization of the IDEA

2015   P.L. 114-95: Every Student Succeeds Act of 2015

Newest reenactment of the ESEA

Increased flexibility in testing for students with disabilities

THE BRAIN

Bernadett Aspromonte

The brain is one of the most complex and interesting areas to learn about in science. Did you know that the brain controls all kinds of actions we can perform, like turning on a light switch or making a sandwich? It also controls how we think and feel. But what is the brain, and what is it made of? What we call the brain is really part of the central nervous system.

Sometimes the brain is described as a computer; it collects, analyzes, processes, sends, and receives a lot of information. However, the brain is much more than just a computer. Just think, a neurosurgeon is able to fix another person's brain with the help of his own. An artist is able to make us think about our lives from a whole different perspective through music, paintings, poems, or sculptures.

Did you know that the brain contains billions of cells that are called neurons? Each neuron has at least ten thousand connections with other neurons. Within those billions of cells and trillions of connections, messages are being sent back and forth to different parts of the brain in the form of electrical signals and chemicals called neurochemicals.

The brain is an organ in your body much like your heart or lungs. It is also part of a system called the central nervous system that is the control center of your body. The brain is made of cells just like any other organ. It contains about a hundred billion neurons. Just to put that number into perspective, there are approximately six billion people living on Earth. That means there are seventeen to eighteen times more neurons in your brain than people living on Earth. The brain also contains other cells called glial cells that feed, maintain, and protect the neurons.

Out of the 100 billion neurons, there are the "big players," the glutamate (more than 20 billion neurons) and GABA neurons (more than 8 billion neurons) and the "fine-tuners," such as dopamine (250,000 neurons), serotonin (250,000 neurons), and norepinephrine (30,000–50,000 neurons) and other neurons like histamine and acetylcholine. The billion-cell systems are doing the main work and the thousand-cell systems are working on the billion-cell systems by fine-tuning them.[1]

In an ADHD brain the fine-tuning system is impaired. The main functions of the brain are less affected, but executive functions and attention to detail seem to

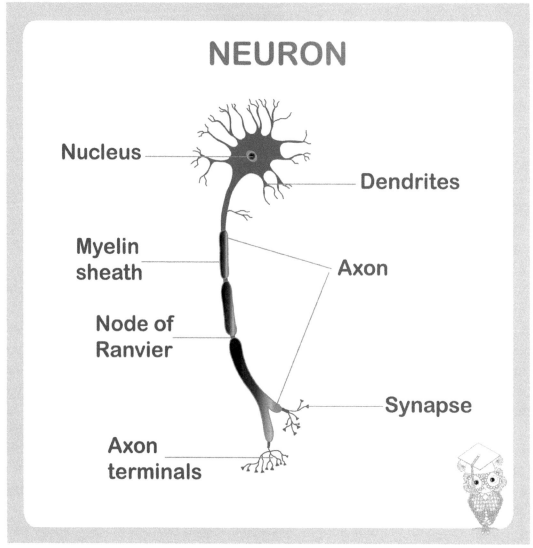

NEURON

Nucleus

Dendrites

Myelin sheath

Axon

Node of Ranvier

Synapse

Axon terminals

The main parts of a neuron. Each neuron has four regions with specific functions: dendrites, cell body and nucleus, axon, and axon terminals forming synapses. © iStock / Dannylyukk

be more altered. When the fine-tuning system is impaired, trying to concentrate can be hard; it's like somebody came in to the room and flipped the switches on all the lights and turned the knobs on all the electronics at the same time. It would be noisy and chaotic, with lights flickering on and off. In this chaos, you probably wouldn't be able to concentrate or do any homework.

Much like in your social life, connections matter. The brain is the most social organ we have. Neurons form networks or neural pathways or circuits. Neural networks are brought to life by electric and neurochemical signaling. The cells of the brain love to connect and chat with each other and gossip. The brain is like Facebook, where the neurons are the members. In 2017, the real Facebook had two billion monthly active users.[2] The human brain has an average of one hundred billion members, the nerve cells. So your brain has up to fifty times more members than Facebook! How many connections do you have on Facebook? The average Facebook user now has about 338 friends.[3] In our brain each nerve cell or neuron has an average of ten thousand connections with other neurons.[4]

The connections where neurons meet are called synapses. Nerve cells can communicate with each other through synaptic and nonsynaptic interactions.[5] Synapses form when nerve cells grow really close to each other, so close they almost touch. This is where synaptic communication happens. The synapse itself consists of the two communicating cell membranes and a gap in between them called the synaptic cleft. Neurochemicals are released into the synaptic cleft and are taken back into the cells. If you multiply the number of neurons by the number of average synapses they each form, you will get one hundred trillion connections or synapses. Through these trillions of connections neurons are able to process a lot of information in a short amount of time. This is called the processing speed.

How can a single nerve cell have so many connections, and how do they send and receive the information from one another? Each neuron has four regions: dendrites, cell body with the nucleus, axon, and axon terminals forming synapses (you can see these in the earlier image). Dendrites are like branches of a tree and they receive information from other neurons through synapses. The incredible variety of dendritic branch shapes makes neurons a more variable, "colorful," and versatile population of cells than any other cell type in our body. A bigger dendritic tree means more synapses, more connections from other neurons. Dendrites pass along the incoming information, and they are also able to process it somewhat. Once the signal reaches the cell body and it is still a strong enough signal, it passes along the axon and gets to the end terminal of the axon, where it turns into a chemical molecule.[6] Neuroscientists say that the biggest scientific challenges of this century will be to connect the function of a single nerve cell to the global operation of the brain.[7]

How Does a Neuron Work?

Neurons are electric, which means that inside the neuron information spreads through its entire body surface from one end to another in the form of electricity. Once this electric signal reaches the very end of the cell, it transforms into chemical molecules, also called neurotransmitters, that exit the cell and swim across the synaptic cleft, between two connecting cells (called the synapse). Certain types of neurons produce certain types of neurotransmitters. For example, some neurons produce glutamate, other neurons produce dopamine, and so on. Once the specific neurotransmitter reaches the next neuron, and if the next neuron is ready to receive new information, the chemical signal turns into an electric signal again.[8]

Electrical signals can run through nerve cells quickly. How quickly? The speed depends on the fatty coating, or electrical insulation, of the nerve cell. This fatty coating is called the myelin sheath. Much like the coating of an electrical wire in your home, the myelin sheath insulates the axon and speeds up the traveling speed of information (electricity) along the axon. The myelin sheath contains breaks called nodes of Ranvier. By jumping from node to node, the electric impulse can travel way faster than if it had to travel along the entire length of the uncoated axon. The thicker the axon is, the faster the electric signal or information travels.

What would happen if the myelin sheath was removed? The consequence would be detrimental and even life threatening. Information would not go as quickly and reliably from neuron to neuron and from one brain region to another or from the brain to the other parts of the body. The more the fatty coating is destroyed, the slower and less efficiently the nerve cells are functioning and the slower and less reliable the information is.

Myelin ensures smooth and fast flow of neuronal information throughout the entire brain. Myelinated axons are connecting relatively distant brain regions and allowing information to be integrated across the entire brain, linking seeing to hearing and speaking to moving. Neural circuits would not function properly without myelin.

Myelination Delay in ADHD

Did you know that myelination is a process? This process continues throughout your entire lifetime up until the age of fifty. Research indicates that myelination is needed for all of those functions that are affected by ADHD, such as high-level cognitive functions and impulse control, something we could summarize as life experience and wisdom.[9] In other words, if you could look inside the brain of master Yoda from *Star Wars*, you would find highly myelinated axons.

Research suggests that in ADHD myelination development is delayed. In the normally developing brain, axon and myelin sheath diameters undergo tremendous growth during the first two years of life but may not fully reach complete maturation before adolescence or even late adulthood.[10]

There is a direct link between myelination and reaction time. Your reaction time is the shortest, meaning that you react the fastest, from the end of adolescence through early adulthood. Then your reaction time increases with age, which means your reactions get slower.[11] However, the reaction time needed to inhibit psychomotor responses and complex behaviors continues improving and peaks between the ages of thirty to fifty-nine, before it declines.[12]

An example of this could be a professional baseball player who can hit faster pitches when he is younger (faster reaction time), and then his swing slows with

---

Did You Know?

Substances such as alcohol and drugs are toxic to the extremely vulnerable myelination process and contribute to the symptoms of ADHD.

---

age. At the same time, baseball players' strikeout percentage goes down as they get older. A reason could be their ability to *not swing* at bad pitches (inhibition of motor responses) and wear pitchers down resulting in more walks.

Between the ages of six and twelve, girls develop impulse control and are able to inhibit hyperactive behavior at a much faster rate than boys. This could explain why girls seems to have much lower rates of ADHD combined.[13]

Delayed Synaptic Pruning in ADHD

The ADHD brain has everything that the non-ADHD brain has. ADHD is considered a neurodevelopmental delay. This means that the ADHD brain goes through the same steps of development in the same order, but these steps take longer. In other words, the development of the brain is delayed somewhat. Scientific research suggests that brain development in children with ADHD is generally delayed by several years compared to children without ADHD.[14] The ADHD brain seems to need more time to ripen.

What does *unripe* or *young* really mean when it comes to the cells of the brain? The young brain looks like a big, overgrown garden of interconnected cells. Neurons need trimming in order to turn the exotic jungle of cells into a nice, well-groomed garden. A young brain has an abundance of dendrites (cellular branches). Dendrites receive synapses and are able to grow out and also grow back based on the incoming information of their environment. Synapses are most often formed between axon terminals and dendrites. If you are a dendrite and receive an overwhelming number of synapses, you need to be able to select which synapse is stronger and, more importantly, which is less likely to work effectively. Trimming of unnecessary synapses, called synaptic pruning, is a natural process that happens in the normally developing brain. This natural, built-in trimming also seems to be delayed in the ADHD brain, by about three years.[15]

There is a delayed cellular "pruning" in ADHD, so what's the big deal? Imagine if you got in your car, turned on the navigation system, and typed in your destination. What if the route that the navigation system gave you included every route at the same time? Every street would get you to the destination, however it may take you forever to get there because of the amount of choices and lack of prioritizing. It would be easier to choose from one or two major roads. More options means more time is needed to decide; fewer options means less time is needed. So in this case, less is more. This is why you need to trim dendrites: to reduce the number of options and speed up decision-making and clarity.

Brain Anatomy

The word *anatomy* is a fancy term for the structure of something, or how it is built. Our nervous system has two major parts: the central nervous system (CNS) and the peripheral nervous system (PNS).

The CNS consists of the brain and the spinal cord. The CNS is the boss. It integrates all the information it receives from the entire body and the external environment, and coordinates and influences the activity of all parts of the body. The CNS is highly protected by bone and special packaging. The brain resides in a bony cave, called the skull. The spinal cord resides in a bony tunnel, called the vertebral tunnel. Both the cave and the tunnel have multiple openings for the nerves that are branching out from the brain (cranial nerves) or the spinal cord (spinal nerves).

The brain and the spinal cord have a special packaging and wrapping system. They are both suspended by their special, multi-layered wrapping tissue, called

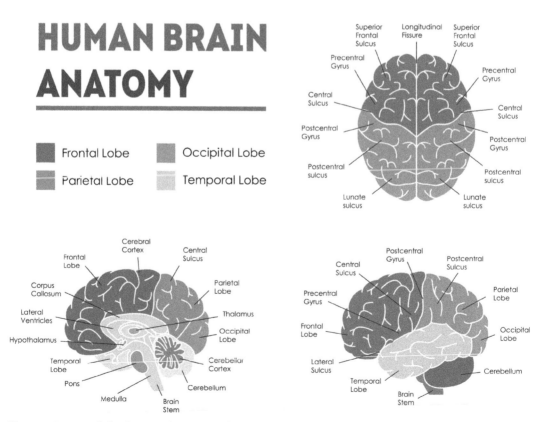

The anatomy of the human brain. Each hemisphere includes four lobes: parietal, occipital, temporal, and frontal. © *iStock / Bigmouse108*

the meninges, and are floating in fluid, called the cerebrospinal fluid. This highly sophisticated suspension system of the meninges and the cerebrospinal fluid absorbs mechanical shocks and protects the brain when we hit our head.

The brain tissue is also isolated from the bloodstream by the blood–brain barrier, which acts as a filter and a border. It serves as border patrol, deciding which molecules are allowed to enter the territory of the brain tissue. Although the brain is highly protected, it is still susceptible to damage, disease, toxins, and infections.

The spinal cord stretches from the base of the skull and terminates about at the level of the first or second lumbar vertebra. The spinal cord occupies the upper region of the vertebral canal.

The peripheral nervous system (PNS) consists of the nerves and groups of neurons called ganglia outside the brain and spinal cord. The PNS connects the CNS to the limbs and organs and serves as a relay between the brain plus spinal cord and other body parts. Unlike the CNS, the PNS is not protected by the vertebral column and skull, or by the blood–brain barrier, which leaves it more exposed to mechanical injuries, infections, toxins, and diseases.

The Brain

The human brain has three major parts: the cerebrum, brainstem, and the cerebellum. The cerebrum is the largest part of the brain. The cerebrum is further divided into two cerebral hemispheres, the right and the left hemispheres, that look like mirror images of one another. Although the left and right hemispheres may look the same, they are not responsible for the same functions. Functions associated with the right side are visual and spatial ability, and functions associated with the left side include language. The hemispheres are connected through bundles of myelinated axons, called the nerve tracts. The thickest bundle of nerve tracts is called the corpus callosum.

Did you know that both the cerebrum and the cerebellum have layers? The outer layer is called the cortex, which is also referred to as gray matter because it has gray color. The cortex gets its gray color because it mostly consists of cell bodies, synapses, and blood vessels and very few axons. The cerebral cortex is responsible for intelligence and consciousness. Underneath the gray matter is the white matter. The white matter mostly consists of myelinated axons. Myelin is a fatty coating that covers axons and is white in color; hence the name white matter. White matter connects the cell bodies of different parts of *gray matter* to each other. Underneath the cerebral cortex we will find several important brain areas, including the amygdala, the hippocampus, and the nuclei of the basal ganglia. These are areas that are all affected in ADHD.

The hemispheres (including the cerebral cortex) are further divided into four lobes: the frontal, parietal, temporal, and occipital (all four lobes can be seen in the image near the beginning of this section). Different lobes are responsible for different functions. Let's see them in detail.

The frontal lobe is located at the front of the brain, right behind the forehead, and is responsible for important motor, cognitive, social, and behavioral functions. The higher cognitive functions include planning, weighing pros and cons, reasoning, self-control, impulse control, spontaneity, abstract reasoning and thought, emotional expression, problem solving, memory, self-expression, judgment, and ethical understanding.

Damage to the frontal lobe can cause a wide variety of symptoms. For example, a person with a damaged frontal lobe would have a hard time reasoning and forming simple thoughts. Damage to the frontal lobe might cause mood changes or difficulty planning speech, thoughts, or motor movements. Size reduction of the frontal lobe was discovered in the ADHD brain.

The parietal lobe is located at the back of the brain and is responsible for integrating sensory and visual information. The parietal lobe receives important sensory information from the rest of the body, such as touch, temperature, taste, and movement. Your parietal lobe is also involved in performing reading and math.

Damage to the left parietal lobe can cause difficulty with writing (agraphia), confusion of right and left side, and problems with math and language. It might also cause problems with perception, for example, difficulty recognizing people, objects, shapes, smells, or sounds.

The temporal lobe is located on the sides of the brain, right behind your temples. This lobe is primarily devoted to hearing. It processes auditory information coming in from your ears. It also plays an important role in creating and recalling certain memories, especially those associated with music. Some parts of this lobe link memories with sound, sight, taste, and touch. Temporal lobe damage affects language and personality.

Damage to or a problem with the temporal lobe might cause a person to find it difficult to place words or pictures into categories. Left-side temporal lobe damage may make it difficult to remember something you have heard or read and make it difficult to recognize words or language. Right-side temporal lobe damage may affect your ability to remember music and drawings or to recall faces.

The occipital lobe is located at the back and the bottom of the brain and is dedicated to vision. The occipital lobe processes incoming information from the eyes, and its job is to correctly understand what the eyes are seeing. Damage to the occipital lobe can cause blindness.

Imaging Equipment: How We Look at and Study the Brain

You may not have a lid on your head but with brain imaging we can look inside and see what is in your mind. There are several ways to look inside the brain, called imaging techniques. Scientists looked at brains under a microscope. The medical history of people with brain injury has also provided important insights about the function of different parts of the brain. Modern science and advancement in technology have given us several tools to learn about the living and thinking human brain. We can group these techniques into two major categories: structural imaging and functional imaging.

Structural imaging includes magnetic resonance imaging (MRI) and diffusion tensor imaging (DTI). Structural imaging gives us a clue about how the brain is built inside through a two- or three-dimensional picture. However, it does not give any information about how active the brain part is or how certain structural abnormalities affect the brain's functioning.

Functional imaging includes functional magnetic resonance imaging, electroencephalography, and magnetoencephalograpy. Functional imaging gives us information about what the brain does in action. It gives us hints about which brain part is active and how active it is while the person is performing a given task.

Neurotransmitters

Dopamine, noradrenaline, serotonin, GABA, and glutamate are neurochemicals that transmit information between cells. If we were to imagine that glutamate (more than twenty billion neurons) and GABA (more than eight billion neurons) were the "big players" in the brain, dopamine, noradrenaline, and serotonin would be the fine-tuners. They are important to ADHD because research shows disturbances and imbalances of the dopamine, noradrenaline, and serotonin systems and neuronal circuits. In other words, in ADHD the fine-tuner system is somehow disturbed.

The dopamine systems provide a wide range of functions in the brain. Dopamine is the "feel-good" hormone, the hormone of ecstasy and reward signaling in the brain, which helps in focusing our attention and controlling some aspects of our motor behavior. The dopamine system is made by a group of nerve cells. The cell bodies of the dopamine-producing neurons, or most of them, are sitting in the midbrain and they send their axons to different parts of the forebrain, where they participate in and contribute to several functions.

Diffusion Tensor Imaging

A new scientific research technique called diffusion tensor imaging (DTI) provides information about white matter structure and axon myelination in more detail. An example of DTI can be seen in the image in this sidebar.

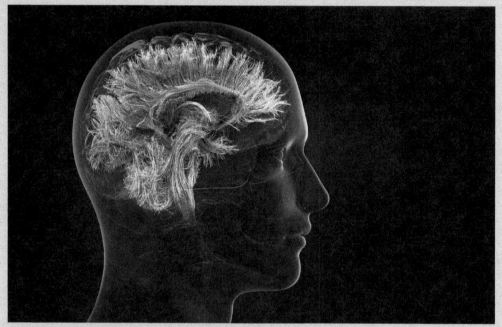

The brain is the most social of all the networks, consisting of billions of nerve cells and trillions of connections and countless pathways in every direction, allowing different areas of the brain to communicate with one another. © *iStock / cosmin4000*

White matter consists of axons (or nerve fibers) covered by myelin sheaths. DTI allows us to "see" nerve pathways (or neural circuits) made by myelinated axons connecting different areas of the brain. A recent study suggests that certain brain circuits may be altered in people with ADHD.[a] DTI studies found abnormalities in the neural circuits of the prefrontal cortex, basal ganglia, brain stem, and cerebellum. Since these areas are involved in attention, impulse control, behavior inhibition, and motor activity, it is not surprising to find that people with ADHD often have hyperactivity, behavioral, attention, and learning problems.[b]

The dopamine system has three main branches. The *thinking* and *remembering* branch goes all the way to the frontal cortex, where it regulates cognitive function and helps you to think and remember more effectively. The *movement* branch reaches to a brain area called the striatum, where dopamine is involved in facilitating movements. In Parkinson's disease, because of loss of dopamine, the movements become rigid and shaky. The third important branch of the dopamine system is the *reward* branch. This branch reaches the limbic system, which is the emotional center of the brain. Within this emotional center you will find an area called the nucleus accumbens, which is the reward center of the brain. Many drugs of abuse exert their effects indirectly or sometimes directly through this reward dopamine system. The dopamine system prepares you for thinking, for movement, and for reward.

The noradrenaline system is involved in arousal or alertness. It is least active when you're asleep, especially when you are dreaming, and it is most active when you are aroused, either moving a lot or thinking a lot. The noradrenaline system is turned on by novelty or new sights and sounds. Too much stimulation, including too much novelty, may cause stress and that may be linked to anxiety. In ADHD the noradrenaline system is affected as well.

Lots of other neurochemicals have been implicated in ADHD. Among them are serotonin, which is one of the oldest and the most mysterious systems in the brain. Serotonin is associated with a number of cognitive disorders, namely, depression, bipolar disorder, and schizophrenia. Researchers have found that certain genetic variations of serotonin receptors[16] or serotonin enzymes[17] increase your risk of having ADHD. Research with rats shows that if rats have low serotonin, they are not able to inhibit their own impulses, which means they are unable to restrain themselves from responding when they should not.[18] Serotonin functions have also been linked to aggression. Low serotonin produces behavioral disinhibition leading to aggression.[19] Disturbances in the serotonin system and/or levels of serotonin in certain brain areas could contribute to ADHD.

Brain Areas Affected by ADHD

The brain differences in people with ADHD are small and subtle. If you look at the brain scans of people living with ADHD and compare them to scans of people who do not have ADHD, you would see small structural and functional differences, and you would see these minor differences only if you looked at the brain scans of hundreds or thousands of people. No brain imaging technique can diagnose ADHD because of the small and subtle brain differences combined with great individual variability.

Brain Regions That Are Smaller in ADHD

- The *frontal lobe* is located at the front of the brain, right behind the forehead, and is responsible for important motor, cognitive, social, and behavioral functions. The higher cognitive functions include planning, weighing pros and cons, reasoning, self-control, impulse control, spontaneity, abstract reasoning and thought, emotional expression, problem solving, memory, self-expression, judgment, and ethical understanding.

- The *basal ganglia* are a group of cell bodies of neurons located beneath the cortex and at the base of the brain. They are strongly interconnected with the brain stem, thalamus, motor cortex, and other motor areas. They are responsible for initiation of involuntary movements such as tremors and ticks, and they regulate balance, eye movements, and posture. The basal ganglia play a crucial role in cognitive and emotional behaviors, including reward and reinforcement, addictive behaviors, and habit formation.

- The *amygdala* is a complex brain structure adjacent to the hippocampus. The word *amygdala* comes from the Greek word for almond. The amygdala is involved in processing emotions, fear conditioning, and the famous fight-or-flight response. It also links bodily sensations and emotions to memories. For example, when the smell of baking cookies in the oven reminds you of a childhood memory, that is your amygdala in action. The amygdala is responsible for autonomic responses associated with fear, arousal, and emotional stimulation. It has been linked to neuropsychiatric disorders, such as anxiety disorder and social phobias. The amygdala is also responsible for fear conditioning.[c]

- The *hippocampus* is an ancient brain region and is closely aligned to memory formation. It is important as an early storage place for long–term memory, and it is involved in the transition of long–term memory to even more enduring permanent memory. The hippocampus also plays an important role in spatial navigation.

- The *corpus callosum* consists of a large bundle of myelinated axons, which connect the right and left hemispheres and allow the two hemispheres to talk to each other. Each hemisphere controls movement on the opposite side of the body.

- The *anterior cingulate cortex* is the frontal part of the cingulate cortex. It is located in between the eyes, deep inside the brain in the midline, on the inner walls of the hemispheres and forms a "collar" surrounding the frontal part of the corpus callosum. It connects to both the limbic system (emotional) and the prefrontal cortex (cognitive). It regulates emotions and pain and is involved in fear and avoidance. It plays an important role in learning how to avoid negative situations and remove the body from the way of harm. Emotional dysregulation in ADHD is associated with the size reduction of this brain area.

- The *brain stem* connects the cerebrum to the spinal cord. The brain stem has three parts: the midbrain, the pons, and the medulla oblongata. It controls vital functions such as breathing, heart rate, and blood pressure. The brain stem organizes motor movements in collaboration with the motor cortex and associated areas.

- The *cerebellum* is connected to the brain stem by its tracts and monitors and regulates voluntary movement and coordinates balance, timing, and sequence learning. Although the cerebellum is only 10 percent of total brain weight, it contains more neurons than the rest of the brain combined. The cerebellum is also famous for being one of the few brain structures where adult neurogenesis (the development of new neurons) has been discovered.[d]

What are the brain areas that are most affected in ADHD? Scientific research shows that there are primarily five brain regions that are affected. These five regions form an interconnected network and the size of this network is directly related to ADHD. The size of these five brain areas is 3 to 10 percent smaller in the ADHD brain. These five areas are the prefrontal cortex (primarily on the right side above the eyebrow), the basal ganglia, the cerebellum, the anterior cingulate cortex, and the corpus callosum.[20]

The prefrontal cortex is a part of the frontal lobe, right behind our forehead. This brain area is responsible for higher brain functions and a variety of complex behaviors, such as reasoning, judgment, planning the future, personality, the ability to suppress responses and thoughts, control focus of attention, reward behaviors, higher-order motor or movement control, and working memory, just to name a few. ADHD researchers found deficits in all of these cognitive functions. The prefrontal cortex is significantly less active in children with ADHD when they are asked to perform certain tasks. The cortex is the outer layer of the brain, also called gray matter, which consists of cell bodies. Research shows that the thicker the cortex, the smarter the person. Probably you heard it before that young people's brains soak up information like a sponge. In this example the sponge is the cerebral cortex. So, the thicker your cerebral cortex is, the smarter you are.[21]

During normal human development, the cortex starts off thin, gets thicker with age, and then reaches the maximum thickness during adolescence. Throughout adolescence it gets thinner again. Thickening as well as thinning is a natural process of cortex development. Cortical thinning in adolescence is the result of myelination and the "use it or lose it" selective cutting back of synapses, also called pruning. These cellular processes create and sculpt neural circuits, including those responsible for cognitive abilities.[22] Current research shows that in ADHD, other brain regions—such as the temporal cortex, parietal cortex, brain stem, hippocampus, and amygdala—are also smaller in volume.[23]

The Late Bloomer Prefrontal Cortex and the Early Bloomer Primary Motor Cortex

Researchers measure the thickness of the cortex across the brain, at certain locations, at a certain age and use these data as a measurement of brain maturation. The main difference that was found in kids with ADHD was the delayed brain cortical thickening, meaning delayed brain maturation. Kids with ADHD reached the same milestones of brain maturation roughly three years later than their non-ADHD peers. The age by which the cortical points reached peak thickness for the ADHD group was 10.5 years, while the average age for the control group was 7.5 years. The brain part that was most delayed was the dorsolateral prefrontal cortex, part of the frontal lobe. It is a highly evolved part of the brain in humans, which matures later than most other regions of the brain.

The dorsolateral prefrontal cortex seems to integrate information from lots of other areas of the brain. This brain region is the highest control center of attention, working memory, and planning. The fact that people with ADHD show developmental delay in this area provides insight into why they also have attention problems and find it difficult to plan ahead. This shows that ADHD is a developmental problem because the brains of kids with ADHD develop in the same order but at a significantly slower pace than normal.[24] The good news is that over time, the ADHD brain could recover from its delay. By the end of adolescence, the frontal lobes in some kids with ADHD have reached normal thickness. This could explain why for some, the symptoms of ADHD are alleviated with age.

During normal brain development the motor cortex and brain stem mature first in children and become fully functional by the time children hit puberty. The frontal lobe is responsible for more complex functions. The frontal lobe is a relatively recent biological invention; it does not finish growing and maturing until the end of the teenage years. During normal brain development the prefrontal cortex is the last brain area to fully mature, and in children with ADHD it just matures a little bit slower. The behavioral problems typically tend to disappear at about the same time as the brain starts to catch up. With age, a person with ADHD may get better at focusing his or her attention and shutting out distractions, so the outside world slowly becomes a less overwhelming place.

These maturational delays were not only found in the frontal lobe but also in the temporal cortex, which is right above the ears. The common feature of the frontal and temporal lobes is that they are interconnected with other cortical regions and integrate information from lower-order sensory areas and feed it to higher-order brain areas that are responsible for control of attention and action. Structural and functional differences of these systems could also explain the sensory processing issues often associated with ADHD.

Interestingly, in contrast to the delay in the frontal and temporal cortex, the primary motor cortex was the only cortical area that showed slightly earlier maturation by two to three years. So the motor cortex, responsible for our moves, is an early bloomer. In a nutshell, in ADHD we have an early-bloomer motor cortex generating hyperactivity and a premature frontal lobe not being able to control it. The late-bloomer prefrontal cortex and the early-bloomer motor cortex causes the excessive and poorly controlled motor activity we see in ADHD.

Medications Used to Treat ADHD

ADHD is often treated with either stimulant or nonstimulant medication. There are two classes of stimulants, those that contain methylphenidate and those that contain amphetamine. Both of these drugs affect dopamine and noradrenaline levels in the brain. Methylphenidate and amphetamine block the reuptake of dopamine into neurons. It is not entirely clear how this reduces the symptoms of ADHD; however about 90 percent of children respond well to these medications.

The nonstimulant medications are a relatively new way to treat ADHD. Antidepressant-like drugs, such as atomoxetine or Strattera, seems to be effective as

The "Chemical Imbalance Approach" to Treat ADHD

The brain is not just a soup of chemicals. The brain produces chemicals, called the neurotransmitters, that are produced and stored inside of neurons. They are released from neurons when they are triggered to release in a timely fashion. These neurotransmitters ensure smooth flow of information from one cell to the next and act at specific sites in neuronal circuits. They act at specific locations, at specific synapses to enable or change the flow of information. The neural information is time and location sensitive. It does matter when and where neurotransmitters are released. So is the chemical imbalance approach to treat ADHD the best one? The traditional view on psychiatric disorders is that they are caused by chemical imbalances in the brain. The drugs designed to treat these problems are in fact changing the global chemistry of the brain. These drugs actually do not work so well for everybody and often fail to provide the ultimate cure. A lot of people would not take these drugs or will stop taking them because of the unwanted side effects or because they simply fail to really help and improve symptoms. These drugs have side effects and those side effects are a problem. "Using them to treat complex psychiatric disorders is like trying to change your engine oil by opening an oil can and poring it all over the engine block; some of it will dribble into the right place but a lot of it will do more harm than good."[e]

well. The idea is that the medication somehow affects how neurons take up noradrenaline and serotonin. Antidepressant drugs were proven to have a protective effect on neurons (neuro protection).[25]

As Dr. Russell Barkley summarizes in his "Stimulants Protect ADHD Brains" talk, stimulants and atomoxetine had proven to have neuro-protective effects in the prefrontal cortex, amygdala, anterior cingulate cortex, basal ganglia, and cerebellum. Dr. Barkley says that drugs for ADHD promote neurodevelopment in these brain areas and normalize the differences present in the ADHD brain.[26]

Although neurotransmitters are an important part of brain functioning, psychiatric disorders are not as simple as general chemical imbalances in the brain but rather disturbances of flow of information through neuronal circuits that are responsible for emotion, mood, and attention. Since the brain is not a soup of chemicals, "it is a mistake to try to treat ADHD for example just by changing the flavor of the soup."[27] We need more research to find better medical treatment for ADHD.

Questions and Answers

Is ADHD Heritable?

Yes, ADHD is heritable. These brain differences are mostly due to genetic differences. Genes involved in transporting and receiving dopamine have been suspected of contributing to ADHD. A number of suspects, called the candidate genes, have been identified, including the dopamine transporter gene and the dopamine 4 receptor gene.[28] ADHD runs in the family. The closer people are genetically related, the higher the risk that if one has ADHD, the other will have it as well. If a parent has ADHD, there is a 40 to 54 percent chance that the children will have it as well. These chances are 25 to 35 percent if you have a sibling with ADHD and 75 to 92 percent between identical twins. If you have ADHD, there is a 20 percent chance that your mother has it and around a 30 percent chance that your father has it as well.

Are There Any Other Factors Contributing to ADHD?

Yes, for example prenatal or neonatal exposure to lead, toxins, smoking, and poor diet can all be factors. If you have a high level of lead in your environment or in your blood, you have a higher risk for ADHD.

How can you get in contact with lead? By breathing or swallowing something with lead in it, such as paint, dust, water, or food. In rare cases streptococcus bacteria can cause ADHD. Unfortunately, the outside protein of the streptococcus bacteria looks like proteins in the brain. When the immune system tries to fight the bacteria, it also attacks the brain because it cannot distinguish the bacteria from neurons. Another contributing factor is smoking. If a mom smokes, the risk of the child having ADHD is higher. The effect of smoking gets worse if the child also has a genetic predisposition for ADHD. This is an interesting and frightening example of how environmental factors, such as smoking and genetic background, have a combined effect on someone's life.

Which Neurotransmitters Are Involved in ADHD?

The neurotransmitters involved are dopamine, serotonin, and norepinephrine. Changes to dopamine levels in the brain and how the cortex develops are closely related. Altered dopamine levels might explain why neurodevelopment is delayed in ADHD. Medications such as methylphenidate (Ritalin) work on dopamine receptors and have an effect on dopamine levels. Serotonin also has to do with ADHD. Researchers are examining the serotonin neurotransmitter in relation to ADHD.

Can We Outgrow ADHD?

Scientific research shows that 33 percent of children with ADHD actually outgrow it while 20 to 25 percent of children with ADHD will continue to have it later in their adult life as well. Approximately 40 percent of children with ADHD will remain somewhere in between.

WHY SCHOOLWORK IS SO HARD (AND WHAT TO DO ABOUT IT)

Educational Statistics

According to research, a third to a quarter of students with ADHD also have learning disabilities.[1] In addition, people with ADHD have higher rates of conduct and mood disorders. Approximately 28 percent of students with ADHD repeat a grade, and over 30 percent do not graduate high school on time.[2] Of the general population, only 5 percent of students with ADHD graduate college compared to around 40 percent of the general population.[3] In addition students with ADHD in college represent 25 percent of the special education services that are provided.[4] Children with ADHD are twice as likely to be suspended from school for discipline reasons and much more likely to be bullied.

When we hear statistics like this we may say to ourselves, "Wow, school does not sound like a great place for students with ADHD, right?" Wrong, school is a great place for kids with ADHD, but it really matters how they approach school and what type of school they go to. How are all these statistics possible if students with ADHD love to learn, are bright, and full of energy? It is not an easy question to answer. Not all students with ADHD have a tough time in school but some will.

When we hear statistics like these we may think that children with ADHD behave poorly or they are not good students or they are not smart, but this is not the case. It comes down to the fact that there are certain expectations that schools place on students, and sometimes there is a mismatch between the expectations of school and what a student with ADHD is able to do.

The statistics listed earlier do not represent all individuals with ADHD. Rather the statistics can be used as tools to help you understand the pitfalls of school, why it is difficult, and what you can do to make sure you have a great school experience.

As we learned in chapter 3 there are ways to get services from your school called modifications and accommodations. We can think of this as what your school can do for you. However, we may also think about what we can do for ourselves. As we get older we should get better at coping with the demands that are placed on us to make our own lives easier. Unfortunately, the statistics on ADHD tell the story of adults with increased unemployment or underemployment, more frequent job changes, and lower college graduation rates. Knowing how to cope with the demands of school is important for you to become a success story.

In addition, success in school does not always equal success in life. Understanding that poor grades in school do not equal failure as a person is important. Only you can define what success is, not someone else. You are a unique and valuable person; your performance in school reflects many factors, but it *does not* reflect on your worth as a person (so don't feel bad if you do not get all As). Many successful people struggled in school.

Albert Einstein, the German-born physicist, is one of the most famous scientists in history. Einstein won a Nobel Prize for his contributions to the field of

A 1947 photo of German-born physicist Albert Einstein, who was noted to have had a difficult time during his school days. *Library of Congress; Photographer: Orren Jack Turner*

physics. It has been reported that he was expelled from school for undermining the authority of his teachers and being a disruptive influence. A teacher described him as "mentally slow, unsociable and adrift forever in his foolish dreams."[5] Albert Einstein later went on to achieve levels of thought and creativity that were unparalleled by almost anyone in human history. How did his teacher not see his potential?

Another example: consider the case of John, who in 1949 attended Eton College and dreamed of becoming a scientist. However, last in his class, he received the following comment on his report card: "His work is far from satisfactory . . . he will not listen, but will insist on doing things his work his own way. . . . I believe he has ideas about becoming a Scientist; on his present showing this is quite ridiculous, if he can't learn simple biological facts he would have no chance of doing the work of a specialist, and it would be a sheer waste of time on his part, and those who have to teach him."[6] The quote is from the report card of Sir John B. Gurdon, winner of the 2012 Nobel Prize in Physiology or Medicine for his revolutionary research on stem cells. Currently he keeps the report card over his desk for amusement.

Like so many other highly creative, competent individuals, Gurdon might have been referred for testing and given the label attention-deficit hyperactive disorder."[7] Sir John later went on to study at Oxford where he claimed he received poor grades because of his difficulty remembering facts and taking notes.[8]

As you will read in chapter 10, there are many successful people with ADHD in many different professions; however, Einstein and Gurdon were chosen for this chapter for a reason. Both were scientists who excelled in the academic world despite having trouble in school. In other words, having trouble in school does not have to stop you from doing anything you want for a living.

Demands of School

Early in school, when we are younger, the demands of school are simple, right? Sit and listen, wait for your turn, follow directions, stand in line, raise your hand, and share. Schoolwork is organized for us and the emphasis is generally on learning basic skills like reading, writing, math, and socializing. The majority of problems that children with ADHD have in lower grades are with following these rules, specifically due to their impulsivity and hyperactivity. Standing in line, waiting for your turn, and not calling out are hard for students with ADHD.

In middle school and high school everything changes. Academically the demands shift more from learning basic skills to learning about content such as history, current events, literature, and more complex math. In addition, teachers and parents begin to expect that you organize your own lives; write down your homework; keep your rooms, backpacks, lockers, and desks clean; manage deadlines for long-term assignments and papers. These are big changes! You are asked

Stephen: An Example of the Demands of School

Stephen is a student in a classroom, who has been asked by the teacher to take out his notebook, turn to the next blank page, write his homework, and put the notebook back in his backpack. Stephen remembered steps 1–3 of the directions and then turned to his friend to ask for the directions again. As Stephen's friend was telling him, the teacher turned around and said, "Stephen, why are you not writing your homework?"

Stephen replied, "Because I did not hear the directions."

The teacher replied, "You should have been listening; look everyone else heard the directions." The class laughed when she said this and Stephen got annoyed and said, "Well maybe you should have written them on the board." The teacher got very angry and sent Stephen to the office.

Stephen may have trouble paying attention and could not remember all the steps to write down his homework because he never heard them in the first place. Because of his teacher's lack of understanding, she thought that he was just choosing to do something other than what he was told. When the teacher compared him to everyone else in the room, who may be better at paying attention and remembering, this made Stephen angry because he thought he was trying to do what he was told, and he impulsively talked back to the teacher, getting in trouble.

This is a great example of how ADHD may look like laziness or defiance in the classroom when it is really a lack of attention.

to rely more on your executive functions described in chapter 1. Much of the support given to you by adults in elementary school becomes your own responsibility. Socially you rely less on parent-organized events and begin to have your own groups of friends. Social demands become more complicated rather than just following rules, sharing, taking turns, and playing in the schoolyard. This is why we have to think about ways to make school experiences easier.

Modifications and Accommodations

An accommodation is meant to *level the playing field*. An accommodation allows a student to complete the same assignment or test as everyone else, but with changes in timing, formatting, setting, scheduling, responding, and/or presenting. Accommodations do not change what is being asked; they make it easier to do the work.[9] All fifty states now have written guidelines to indicate which accommodations can be used.

A modification, on the other hand, somehow changes, lowers, or reduces the expectation. Examples include learning less material, reducing assignments, and being graded using different standards. A modification also makes work easier, however, by changing what has to be learned.

Accommodations and modifications can help adapt the way a book or material is presented to you, change your classroom environment, make directions easier to follow, help you manage time, make writing easier, make grading more meaningful, help with tests, help with math, or give you tools that help to do your work.[10] Examples of accommodations include the teacher providing the following:

- Two sets of textbooks, one for home and one for school
- Audio book
- A list of page numbers to help find answers
- Alternatives for written assignments
- Examples of correctly completed work
- An early syllabus
- Preferred seating
- Clear or printed directions
- Increased transition time
- Notes or a notetaker
- Allowance for assignments to be reworked
- Daily grades incorporated into final grade
- Open book test exception
- Extended time for tests
- Alternate assessments

Examples of modifications include the following:

- Being allowed to read easier books with lower reading levels
- Having modified expectations after assignments (list three main points) instead of a test
- Having a reduced number of assignments or a different assignment to make them easier to complete
- Having an alternative grading system based on effort or personal growth
- Having the teacher change classroom rules for the student

Jay Leno

Comedian Jay Leno describes an accommodation that he made for himself while hosting *The Tonight Show* to help him with his difficulty reading due to dyslexia. "I tend to use cue cards rather than a teleprompter, because with the cue cards, you can put the whole phrase on the card, whereas the teleprompters go only two or three words at a time, but when I see a cue card, I see the whole thing all at once and I will sometimes paraphrase."[a] This is an example of a presentation accommodation. It did not change the joke that Jay had to tell, but rather how that joke was presented to him so that he could effectively deliver it to the audience.

Some accommodations are more helpful, especially for students with ADHD. These may include (1) brief academic or behavioral instructions that are written down or posted in a visible area; (2) rewards or consequences posted for good behavior in class; (3) special help from teachers when changing classes or periods; (4) special help from teachers to let the student know when he has met his goals; (5) teachers giving rewards to a student when she has done a great job.[11]

Academy Award–winning director Steven Spielberg has talked about having dyslexia and his struggles reading. *Universal Pictures / Photofest © Universal Pictures*

Obtaining accommodations and modifications can be done through your school and are listed on individual education programs (IEPs). However not all accommodations need to be on an IEP; some accommodations can be used at the discretion of your teacher. These are called universal accommodations. Examples of universal accommodations are preferential seating, reading the directions out loud, or giving extra encouragement. So it doesn't hurt to ask your teacher for help.

Ways You Can Help Yourself

What has been listed here are ways that your school can help you to succeed academically. However there are also ways that you can help yourself to do your best in school. What follows is a guide to fitting in to the way that most schools operate. I am not suggesting that you agree with the current model of how most schools operate. Sitting for hours in front of a lecture or book is no way to learn, at least not for me. Personally, I think learning should be interactive, fun, and based on projects and experimentation. Learning should foster a love of finding out why or how something works using your creativity and energy to solve problems. However, sometimes hitting the books is necessary to get thorough school. Sometimes it is also necessary to sit for extended periods and listen to lectures.

So take the suggestions in the following paragraphs as more of a guide for fitting the brilliantly creative smart and fun round peg (that is you) into the boring square hole that is sometimes school.

Areas that are difficult for students with ADHD include

- paying attention in class
- taking notes
- organizing
- doing homework
- studying
- taking tests

Paying Attention in Class

If you're like most people with ADHD you may not appreciate it if someone tells you to "pay attention." Would you tell someone with polio to "stand up straight and walk properly?" Probably not. Paying attention in class can be difficult, especially if the material is not very interesting and you don't need to be reminded of it. Let's face it, sometimes class is super boring, but that is a fact of life. There are strategies you can use to help stay engaged in class.

Ask questions to remain engaged in the class discussion. If you frequently participate in class, the teacher will know that you are paying attention. You will be considered "a participator," which is good. Soon the teacher may look to you for comments. The teacher will have a positive opinion of you when it comes to your class participation. The teacher will know that you have been involved in the class discussions from day one. Even if you receive poor grades on tests often teachers take class participation into account when grading. Teachers will remember that you had listened and commented on the topics. This can help when a teacher grades you. I have heard teachers say many times when grading a test, "How did you get this question wrong? You told me the answer to this in

Case Study

Sandra is a fifteen-year-old girl diagnosed with ADHD inattentive type. When Sandra is in class she is often looking at the teacher, has her notebook in front of her, and appears to be following the lesson. Sandra is not calling out, interrupting the teacher, or talking to her friends during class. If you walked into the room during the class, Sandra would look like one of the model students. Her behaviors are not easy to spot because they are the *lack of behavior.*

What is not immediately apparent is that Sandra is often not attending to the teacher for long periods. Her mind is wandering. She is thinking about what she is going to eat for lunch, what the girl next to her is wearing, and what she will do when she gets home that night. She is noticing lots of things around the room such as classmates moving in their seats, the sound of the air conditioning, and noises in the hallway.

Sandra appears to be taking notes, however the notes that she takes are missing many of the details that the teacher is giving. Sandra's notes are not organized; they are missing information even though her handwriting may look nice. Sandra's notes will not be very useful when studying for a test.

During class there are others in the room who are calling out or talking to their neighbors or even texting during class. When the teacher gets upset, these are the students that the teacher focuses on—the ones who are disrupting the room. Rarely does the teacher pay any mind to Sandra because she is not causing any trouble. When the teacher grades Sandra's test, he is confused about how she did so poorly. This shows that ADHD is not always about hyperactivity and impulsivity. Sometimes it is the student teachers don't even notice.

class." One note: class participation is great, but it must be done according to the rules of the class. This includes raising your hand, waiting to be called on, and taking turns in the class conversation.

Know when to focus, and when not to. It is nearly impossible to be sitting on the edge of your seat for forty-five minutes when listening to a lecture on chlorophyll, when it sounds more like borophyll! As we discussed in chapter 1, students with ADHD don't have trouble paying attention; they pay attention to everything! Focusing attention for short periods of time is easier than longer periods. Focusing attention for forty-five minutes may not be possible but forty-five seconds may be. This is the key, small bundles of information when it counts. Every class differs, but teachers generally give signs when something is *really important*, and you should write it down. When a teacher is shuffling through papers at their desk, not so important; when they write something on the board, probably important. Learn when to zero in and get the important info during class and take a mental rest in between.

Taking Notes

Did you know that the quality of one's notes is one of the biggest predictors of academic success?[12] And one of the biggest predictors of note quality is note-taking speed.[13] Taking notes is not easy; in fact, it is very difficult.

When I was in high school I had a history class with a teacher who used to write all of the class notes on the chalkboards in the classroom in six-point font. These notes covered information we would need to take the next test. We would walk into the room and immediately begin copying off of the boards. During class he would lecture about the content of the boards. At the end of the week everyone would line up at his desk, and he would grade our notes on the spot (handwriting included). This is a worst-case scenario for anyone who has trouble taking notes.

Organizing and writing notes can be very difficult for anyone. Lapses in attention or motivation can make it even harder to keep a flow and organization to your notes. Some teachers give out the notes before class. This is a great accommodation and can be very helpful. Some teachers require you to take and organize your own notes, which is not so great. Some teachers teach directly from the book. Although this may be boring, it can actually help with organization of notes. Here are some suggestions for taking notes:

- Take notes the best that you can and also share the responsibility with a friend: before class, decide who will take notes on each section. Jot down important points if you can't keep up. Do not sacrifice your understanding just to write, especially if someone is willing to share the responsibility with you.

- If you know that a teacher teaches directly from the book, photocopy the chapters beforehand and highlight the chapters as the teacher progresses. No need to reinvent the wheel or spend time writing feverishly when the teacher is reading from the book.
- Use technology. I would not suggest audio recording every class because it is too time-consuming to listen to. However, for important info use the tech; it can be a big help. Snap a pic of the notes on the board or record a small portion of a lecture, especially when the teacher gives homework.

Organization

Organization in general is hard for individuals with ADHD. Let's focus on school-work, though. Sometimes people with ADHD are not organized in their heads; too many thoughts come too quickly and without structure. This can be one of the great things about ADHD as it contributes to creativity and imagination, but not so much for keeping assignments organized.

If you cannot organize something in your own head, take it out of your head and organize it on paper (or your phone). The answer here is to make lists; make as many lists as possible. Use a calendar and also plan ahead. There is an old expression that goes, "If you have eight hours to cut down a tree, spend the first four hours sharpening your ax." This logic can be applied to planning your day. Spend some time planning your day; don't just attack it. Making lists, reviewing your calendar and schedule, and even packing your backpack every night (when you are not in a rush) are great ways to sharpen your ax for the next day.

Spending time organizing can help you keep routines and make life predictable. Organization and predictability are essential for remembering things, leaving on time, not being late, finishing tasks, and not being in a rush. In addition, being organized can help keep your immediate surroundings clean and functional.

For example, when your room is a total disaster, it's difficult to do anything there. So, instead of doing your homework at your messy desk, you go to the kitchen table to do it, but your notebook is somewhere in your *backpack mess* so you use scrap paper, and when you get to school the next day, guess what—you don't know where the paper is. Sound familiar? Keeping your surroundings clean, organized, and functional can be the difference between completing your work and not completing it.

Homework

Organizing your homework and schoolwork is not easy. Having been a teacher myself I always valued when students would come to ask me questions after

Make It a Habit to Be Organized

Common things to keep organized include your

- room
- backpack
- locker
- car
- desk

Making a habit out of being organized means working on a predictable schedule and building good behaviors that you do on a regular basis to keep your stuff organized. Forming a habit doesn't take a set amount of time; it could take weeks or months. Habits can be helpful because when you do something instinctively, you no longer have to remember to do it.

Good habits include morning routines for getting ready for school, healthy eating at regularly scheduled times, and consistent sleeping schedules. New situations require flexibility and time to build good habits. Spend some time building your own good habits, put your lists in visible places, keep your things organized, and you will begin to limit the forgetfulness that you may experience. This includes routines and schedules. Having a predictable schedule makes getting through the week easier. If you go to bed on time, then you wake up on time, you get to school on time, and you are not tired throughout the day.

class or on their own time. It showed me that they were genuinely interested in the material and they cared about getting the info right. During the school day the schedule is tight and there is often little extra time. I have found it helpful to ask a teacher after school to confirm that notes are complete or look at a written homework assignment, or to ask questions about the homework that you did not think of during the day. Many teachers will give out helpful hints as well during that time. This can help prevent incorrectly completed assignments (that is, assignments where you did not really give the teacher what she wanted), situations where you did the wrong page number or wrote the questions down wrong or did more (or less) work than you had to. Confirm, confirm, confirm.

Have you ever wondered why it was so hard to pay attention in class? Maybe you thought the subject was not interesting or the teacher was boring. Maybe your teachers think you are just lazy or not a very good student. Inattention can look like daydreaming, and it is also part of ADHD. © *iStock / maurusone*

Keep a network of friends. Do not be a lone wolf when studying. Make sure you keep in touch with your friends and classmates about assignments, notes, homework, and studying for tests. This can ensure that you are on the same page as everyone else about what is due and what will be on tests. If you forget something, they remind you; if they forget something you remind them. Divide the work.

Studying

The act of studying. First let me say ugh. Different subjects require different game plans. Studying is kind of easy when it is a very interesting topic. I remember when I was a student I had to study how a tsunami works. I had a choice: I could study a diagram in a textbook or I could find my own resources on how tsunamis work. It is fascinating how they operate. I found videos and TV shows with really great computer simulations. I was riveted to the screen, and I watched them over and over. In fact, many of Earth's natural occurrences were fascinating to me as a student: earthquakes, tornadoes, tsunamis. I also learned so much about geology, oceanography, weather, physics, biology, and science in general, and it was fun. For me, this was real learning. When studying takes on this form, it is unstoppable; learning happens at lightning speed, and the facts stick with you forever. You feel satisfied with the learning, and proud of yourself. But sometimes we have to study topics that others choose (a fact of life), and it may not be so interesting. How do we make it through the studying? Here are some general guidelines that can help:

Stay on track. Know what you are going to do before you do it. If we had un-limited time to study, we would start on chapter 1 and page 1 and read it straight through, maybe twice. But if you have a limited time to study or a limited atten-tion, have a plan before you start so that every minute counts. This is why you should go to teachers to help get your assignments and study sessions organized.

Use a schedule. Schedule when you will study. If you have to learn a chapter of biology by next week, then you may have to study thirty minutes a day for five days; put it on the calendar. Places you have to be and times you have to be at those places—put it on the calendar. Learn to distinguish between tasks that are important and need to be done quickly, important and do not need to be done quickly, not important but need to be done quickly, and not important and do not need to be done quickly. Distinguishing among these categories can help you prioritize your schedule.[14]

Know your limits. If you know that you can only study effectively for an hour, then only study for an hour at a time. If you need to take breaks during that hour, then do it. This means taking breaks before the mental gas tank is empty. By taking breaks you can get an extra study session in or make a session more useful. Take a true break and think about something else; do something completely different for twenty minutes and turn your attention away from the work you are doing.

Chip away at it. Rome wasn't built in a day. Studying and learning is a daily struggle and believe me, the struggle is real. You have to have patience and chip away at assignments to get them done—especially in high school when there are more tests and more long-term assignments than middle and elementary school.

Dave Farrow

Dave Farrow is a two-time Guinness World Record holder in memory, having memorized a random sequence of fifty-nine separate packs of cards (3,068 cards) on a single sighting. The attempt took four hours, fifty-eight minutes, twenty seconds, not including breaks.[b] Dave was diagnosed with ADHD at age fourteen and attributes his memory to practicing techniques that included short and intense bursts of attention with breaks.

They cannot be done in a night or with a single cramming session. Use your calendar to schedule.

Research by Angela Duckworth at the University of Pennsylvania has suggested that getting good grades and succeeding in life can be more attributed to the idea of grit than anything else, including scores on IQ tests, social intelligence, good looks, physical health, or even talent. Grit or grittiness can be described as "stick to it'ness" or persistence, an ability to tolerate frustration to achieve long-term goals. To do this keeping perspective is important. Learning is a process; it takes time and is very difficult. Learning will involve successes and failures and sticking to it over the long term is the only way to get better at it.[15]

Taking Tests

Taking tests is its own special kind of misery for every student. Let me first say this: tests can be very useful tools for educators; they can tell us what someone knows and what they need to learn and give us information to help students learn better. Tests can also be terribly misused by educators. Tests are misused when they are simply given to obtain a score from students in order to give them a grade on their report card.

When tests are used in this way they can lead to test anxiety, fear of failure, nervousness, and most importantly studying and learning for the purpose of taking a test instead of for the purpose of learning. Unfortunately we live in a society that uses tests all the time: tests to put us in a certain class, to tell us if we pass or fail, to compare us to our peers, to get into college, and even to drive.

A test can only give someone a sample of your knowledge at a particular moment, and there are many factors that go into performance on a test besides knowledge of the material: confidence in your knowledge, writing ability, test-taking ability, how well you slept the night before, if you ate breakfast, and so on. For example, an essay test for a history class tests not only your knowledge of history but also your ability to recall and summarize. Multiple-choice questions are testing inductive reasoning and test taking abilities, time management, ability to work under pressure and concentrate for long periods, sometimes without a break. Not to mention the list of times you are at your best probably does not include last period in math class, crammed into a room with twenty other students. Studying for a test is only half of the battle; performing on the test is the other half. As described earlier, having accommodations or modifications can help in this area and these are things your school can do for you.

There are whole books and series that focus on test taking; however there is some practical advice for your state of mind before you take a test. Physiological arousal or test anxiety can increase your performance on tasks, but only until a certain point. After all, being motivated and having a little bit of anxiety can keep us focused and on track. If we walk into a test not caring at all, we may lack the motivation to do well. The other side of that coin is having too much test anxiety. Too much test anxiety can harm your performance. Extremely high states of arousal can make even easy tasks more difficult. Taking tests fits into this example. A little bit of test anxiety can help your performance on a test. Finding your maximal performance zone is something that you can find through practice, especially when you study.

Staying Motivated

Believe it or not there are things that you can do to make schoolwork and studying more interesting, exciting, or motivating. Of course some subjects are very boring, but there are things you can do to make them more interesting, so you can stick to it:

- Have a goal
- Keep it just right
- Give yourself feedback
- Be curious
- Own it
- Use your imagination
- Help each other
- Be at your best
- Get your sleep
- Keep Track
- Don't procrastinate
- Prepare for class

Have a goal. An activity that goes on forever with no end and no goal is not motivating. Know how long you will study for and what your goals are while studying. Whether your goal is to read twenty pages, to make flash cards, copy your class notes, or to finish your homework, know how long and what you would like to study.

Keep it just right. Imagine if we got every answer right on a quiz, or even every answer wrong. Always getting every answer right would be boring and every answer wrong would be too hard; you would not want to do either activity for very long. The key is to challenge yourselves but still be successful.

A great way to do this when studying is by using flash cards. Making flash cards is also a great way to study. If we got every flash card right we would stop;

if we got every card wrong, we would stop too. Make your flash cards and keep the ratio about 50 percent. When you get a lot right, add some more hard ones in. This will keep the flash cards just difficult enough to keep you interested.

Give yourself feedback. Imagine cooking a meal and never tasting it. How would you know if it was any good? Or taking a test and never knowing your score. How would you know how you did? It is no different when you are studying; give yourself feedback so you can stay positive and keep encouraged to go on. Video games use feedback all the time, by giving points or money. Give yourself rewards and praise (or candy) when you are studying so when things get difficult you remember that you have been making progress. Put a check on your calendar to remind yourself that you did it. This can help you maintain confidence and persistence when working.

Be curious. Curiosity can be a double-edged sword. It is a great motivator but can also get you off track at times. This is not to say that curiosity cannot be harnessed; it can help you discover things about subjects that interest or surprise you. We can write down our curiosities and thoughts about a subject as we are reading, for example, how a subject relates to something else we know. We can also structure our study sessions to start with the topics we are most curious about (to give us a kickstart) or to end with them (to keep us motivated).

Own it. Having control over your studying can give you a sense of ownership and responsibility and increase your motivation. Take control of your studying, organize your session, make it your own. Give yourself choices in how you want to approach the task. You can get it right and feel like you have accomplished something.

Use your imagination. Early research on video games found that fantasy created motivation for players to play games. This may seem impossible in studying, but let your imagination go to work. Try making metaphors, analogies, or stories related to the material that you have studied. These strategies can help create motivation and also aide in memory. Set your mitosis steps to your favorite song lyrics, imagine your favorite TV show characters interviewing a historical figure, imagine what would happen if a historical figure went to the mall. Use your creativity and imagination to help you remember.

Help each other. Cooperation, competition, and recognition are all powerful interpersonal motivators that can help you remain motivated to stick with studying. Working together with friends, keeping each other motivated, and congratulating each other on a job well done can build a sense of community when studying and doing work. Having a group of friends to do work with can help keep you motivated when you do not want to do something. Likewise when your friends don't want to study, you can keep them motivated; two heads are better than one.

Be at your best. Being at your best differs from person to person; time of day, meals, exercise, and medication can all affect when you are learning at your best.

Think back to all of your best study sessions. Were they in the morning, afternoon, or evening? Were they after meals or perhaps after a nap? How about the amount of sleep you got the night before; was it good sleep? What about the location: was it a familiar place or a different place, bedroom, living room, or library? Were there distractions, such as other people, or was it quiet? Were you in a good mood? The best study situation is different for everyone. Think about when you are at your best and try to re-create this scenario when you study. In other words, know how to get to your best.

Get your sleep. This sounds like common sense, doesn't it? Did you know that teenagers require at least nine to ten hours of sleep a night?[16] When you are growing you need sleep. You brain uses sleep to process information and consolidate memory.[17] With good sleep your executive functions, memory, and recall will be at their best. In order to remember new information, you better get your sleep. Did you know that it has been reported that between 25 and 50 percent of children with ADHD have sleep problems? This means that getting sleep should be a priority, so no all-nighters; get your sleep to remember.[18]

Keep track. It is easy to get down on yourself, so you need to keep it real. You will have good days and bad days, keep a log so during the bad days you remember that there were good days. Also, what works and what doesn't when you study. You don't need to reinvent the wheel, if it works make a note and do it again.

Don't procrastinate. Making a schedule is important because it holds us to a standard. If we only studied when we were "in the mood," we would not be well prepared for school. Some people may use indecision or confusion to procrastinate because they believe it reduces their responsibility. Some people may procrastinate because they feel they need the rush of a fast-approaching deadline. Some people procrastinate because they feel like a lack of effort is easier to accept than the potential of failing. Whatever your reason is for procrastinating, let your schedule tell you when to start, do your best, and then stop studying.[19]

Prepare for class. This one is hard, but if you kind of know what is coming the next day, review it. Flip through the chapter or reading the night before; then it will seem like more of a review than new info. This can make it easier to pay attention and take notes. It will also make it easier to come back to the work if you lose your attention.

SOCIAL AND EMOTIONAL ASPECTS OF ADHD

Impulsivity is defined in chapter two as a behavior that you do without thinking things through. This can be a difficult aspect of having ADHD. As we look at emotions in this chapter we will learn that emotional impulsivity is also a part of ADHD. Emotional impulsivity is similar to the impulsivity that was described in chapter 1. It's like having very fast emotional reactions without thinking them through. This can make people feel uncomfortable or make them think that you are angry or sad or overly excited.

Reacting emotionally can affect you socially if people do not understand why you behave that way. It can affect your ability to make and keep friends. But don't worry; remember that simply knowing this information can help you. Maybe you can tone down a reaction, tell people in advance that a topic makes you angry, or apologize when you think that you have made someone feel uncomfortable. These are good social-emotional skills. Practicing social-emotional skills is not about being perfect, because no one is perfect. It is about understanding how ADHD affects your social interactions and emotions. Practicing good social-emotional skills can help you make and keep friends.

Social-Emotional Aspects of ADHD

In this chapter we will talk about how ADHD can affect us socially and emotionally. I know what you may be thinking: "Are we going to have to talk about our feelings?" Well, the answer is kind of. It is important to understand the impact that ADHD can have on our (and others') feelings because knowing where our feelings come from can help us not get so mad, sad, or worried about things. In other words, just knowing why we feel the way we do sometimes can really help out when we get upset.

> ## ! Name Your Feelings
>
> - Joy
> - Sadness
> - Anxiety
> - Anger
> - Disgust
> - Shame
> - Pride

When we talk about social and emotional topics we are talking about how we feel about life and ourselves and also how we interact with others and also how they feel and interact with us. Social and emotional topics are very important to people with ADHD. Just like learning about math can make you better at math, learning about how you feel, and why, can make you better at life. Learning about the impact ADHD has on your feelings can give you an advantage. For example, being able to put a name to a feeling and why you are having it can help you understand it better. Understanding the way you feel before you feel it can help you avoid situations that will upset you or help you deal with it better.

When we talk about feelings we are referring to joy, sadness, fear (anxiety/ worry), anger, and disgust. There are also other feelings such as embarrassment, shame, or pride. Being able to accurately name your feelings is important because mislabeling them can lead to confusion about why you are upset.

It is also important to be able to understand appropriate levels of feelings. A great way to practice this is to put your feelings on a scale of one to ten or a thermometer.

Oftentimes you may have the appropriate feeling but it is way too intense for a situation. In other words, on a 1-to-10 scale, you feel angry at a 10, when a 4 would be more appropriate. For example, if you forget your homework at home, screaming, yelling, stomping your feet, and throwing things when you get to school would be an overreaction. These are indicators of an intense emotional reaction, like a ten. Not only is a 10 too much in this situation, it will not get you what you want. Maybe you are mad because you worked hard on the assignment. Maybe you are mad because you do not want to get in trouble or receive a bad grade. Maybe there is a consequence for not handing in your homework. Acting very angry will not get you what you want. Getting a little bit angry and then calmly telling your teacher you left the assignment at home may lead to the teacher taking it easy on you or giving you a second chance. Thinking things through before getting upset can help you get what you want.

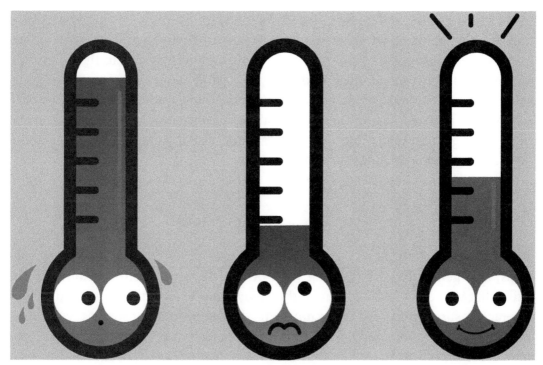

Think of your feelings as being on different thermometers. The more strongly you feel an emotion, the hotter the temperature. Strong feelings have intense reactions. © *iStock / stockakia*

For example, imagine you are in the schoolyard and did not get picked to play a game or got picked last. Would you get angry if this happened to you? How angry would you get? If the goal was to be picked for the game, getting really angry and saying mean things definitely would not get you what you wanted. If you wanted to get picked for the game, you may say, "I waited to play and now it's my turn." However, if you got angry at a 10 because you did not get picked you probably would not get picked the next time either.

Intense feelings lead to intense reactions, and having intense reactions does not get you what you want. It takes practice to identify our feelings. If you act like it is the end of the world in everyday situations, you may be overreacting. You can practice stopping and thinking: when you feel an intense emotion, stop; think about a response that will get you what you want.

Think about all the times you had extreme feelings over the course of the past week. Would you still react in the same way? A good way to rate whether a feeling was consistent with a situation is to put it in perspective. Was the event so bad? Was the event better or worse than something else? For example, let's say you flunked a test and got very angry. You threw your textbook across the room and cursed at the teacher. Of course, this is an extreme reaction. You were mad at the moment. What if you practiced stopping and thinking when you got angry. Failing a test is not what you wanted, but it could be worse. You got an OK grade on the last test and have one more left. Also you have been working with the teacher to get better grades, and he may give you some extra credit. This kind of stopping and thinking could easily turn an angry 10 into an annoyed 5. This is the difference between throwing a book across the room and getting sent to the office, and having a chance to get a better grade. If you only get angry at a 5 and give yourself a minute to think, you may say to yourself, "This grade stinks, and I studied too. Maybe I can ask the teacher for extra credit on the test. Maybe everyone else in the class got bad grades too. Maybe I can still raise my grade." Thinking about your feelings can help you get what you want.

Social Skills

When we talk about social skills we mean making friends, having conversations, and generally getting along with others. If we were to list some of the skills that we need to make friends, they may include initiating or starting social interactions, reciprocating or taking turns during interactions, and terminating or ending interactions. ADHD affects social skills when initiating because you may come on too strong when first meeting someone, go right into a conversation without properly introducing yourself, or insert yourself into an ongoing conversation. Even when you mean well, these actions may make people feel uncomfortable or annoyed.

Be Aware of Social Skills

Do you

- make eye contact when greeting someone?
- take turns during conversations?
- interrupt when speaking to someone?
- share with others?
- change conversation topics without asking others?
- watch the facial expressions of others?
- make eye contact when speaking to someone?
- ask people politely to move out of the way?
- avoid social situations because they make you nervous?

When reciprocating or taking turns, you may interrupt during conversations, disagreeing with people impulsively instead of stating disagreements nicely or with tact. When playing games, you may not share the ball or take turns. When you do not take turns in conversation or playing games, people will not want to deal with you.

Finally, during termination or ending interactions you may walk away without ending the conversation nicely. All of these behaviors can add up to social problems. When we are very young these skills are not always expected, but when we get older, they are. If you do not practice good social skills, you could negatively affect your ability to make and keep friends.

Just because you know a social rule (like taking turns) does not mean that you always do it. Although you know that you are supposed to take turns during a conversation, you still don't; you may know that you are supposed to raise your hand in class but don't. After enough people do not talk to you or enough teachers get annoyed with you for not following social rules, you may decide to stop trying because you know it does not end well. This will definitely not get you what you want. Luckily all social skills can be practiced and knowing is half the battle.

Social Rules

Much like the education laws we talked about in chapter 3, we live by certain rules. The law is very black and white in this respect. Stealing is bad, hurting others will get you in trouble, driving too fast will get you a ticket. But there are other rules in life that are not always so easy to understand. These other rules are rarely if ever written down, and you probably wouldn't read them if they were. These other rules are called social rules. These are the unspoken rules regarding how we act around others. These are rules by which we live our lives every day, and usually we never discuss them with anyone.

For example, if you walked into a room full of chairs with only one other person in that room, would you sit right next to him or her? Probably not. You may sit one or two chairs away or maybe farther. How about asking an adult how old he is? This is OK in some cultures and not OK in others. How about looking someone directly in the eyes when you are talking to her? Again, OK in some cultures and not OK in others. What about how close you stand to someone when speaking to him? Some people like more personal space and others less. How about taking turns in a conversation, not interrupting, asking others to repeat themselves, walking away mid-conversation? What about overposting on social media or sending too many texts to someone? All of these topics fall under social rules, and these types of rules differ from age to age and culture to culture. There are no one-size-fits-all social rules to follow. In order to be social and make friends you must know which social rules to apply and when to apply them.

Sometimes, having ADHD can make it appear as if you are not following these social rules—not because you don't care, but because of impulsivity or hyperactivity. What can happen when you don't follow social rules? It can affect how people treat you, which can affect how you feel about yourself.

When you are very young the result of not following these rules like sharing is that you get in trouble with your parents or teachers. This could make you angry because you do not understand the rules that you broke. You may yell or act out in response. Your parents might try to teach you the rule over again. When you get older you may grab or not share. You may understand the social rules and instantly wish you could take your action back. Or you may not understand what causes you to feel ashamed or embarrassed about your actions. When you become an adult and break social rules, others may choose not to say anything out of politeness, but they may not want to be around you. If you do not understand why, you may become sad or anxious. In this way your behaviors can have an impact on your feelings. Don't worry, knowing is half the battle and social rules can be learned and practiced.

A Bank Account

What does all this have to do with our emotions? It may help to think that the social interactions, feelings, and thoughts you have are like deposits and withdrawals from a bank account. Positive social interaction—a smile, a "great job" from someone—put a dollar in the bank. A "great to see you" or a hug, put two dollars in the bank. A birthday party with all of your friends, gifts, and cards put $100 in the bank. Days like these can leave us feeling great with all the deposits we have made into the bank. What about a negative interaction? For example, "No, that's not right." Take out a dollar. "I told you not to do that." Take out another dollar. "No, why don't you listen?" Take another dollar. The more negative social interactions we have, the less emotional currency we have in the bank and the worse we feel. I am not suggesting that we should care what others think so much that it ruins our day, but having lots of negative social interactions can make us feel bad. The more positive interactions we have, the better we will feel.

When we have lots of negative social interactions, we can feel mad or anxious or sad. We can even start to tell ourselves negative things like "I can't do anything right" or "I should have done a better job" or maybe "I am better off not interacting at all, so I'll avoid that situation." When we do not fit into other people's expectations it can set us up for negative interactions with them and also the world. It is not important to always fit into others' expectations and to always have positive interactions with people. It is important for you to understand if any of your negative interactions are affected by ADHD and if you can do anything about it.

Examples of Social-Emotional Skills

Persistence—the ability to stick to a task even when it is difficult

Frustration tolerance—the ability to cope with a situation that is difficult

Decision making—making good social and emotional decisions and understanding social consequences

Resiliency—the ability to be flexible emotionally and "bounce back" even when something negative happens

Confidence/self-acceptance—having a positive and realistic view of yourself[a]

Social-Emotional Skills

Schools are beginning to teach social-emotional skills and also target skills like getting along with others, social problem solving, and relationship skills. Social-emotional skills are things that you can learn and practice and equally important is knowing when to use them.

For example, imagine you interrupt someone during a conversation and at that moment you call a time-out and ask yourself if you knew that it was wrong to interrupt someone. Most likely your answer would be "Yes, of course I know it is rude to interrupt someone." Well why did you do it then? Most likely it was an impulsive comment; you couldn't wait, or you thought you would forget your answer, or you were so excited that you couldn't wait to say it. In other words, you know interrupting is rude; you just didn't do it right. Most likely you know that waiting for someone to finish a thought is the right thing to do before making a comment and you probably can do it too. But it is hard to do in real life sometimes. In other words you know the rule and have acquired the skill, but cannot perform it because of impulsivity.

You can acquire a skill but fail to perform it when necessary.

Fact: Did you know that the world record holder for free throws is not an NBA basketball player, but a fifty-four-year-old soil conservation technician who made 2,371 free throws in an hour?[1] Did you know that NBA basketball players have not gotten any better at shooting free throws in the last fifty years? Really. The average is 69 percent. If you are unfamiliar, a free throw is when the referee hands the basketball to a player standing behind a line fifteen feet from the basket, and he gets a free shot. Many basketball players shoot much higher percentages of free throws in practice than they do in games. Why is this? Learning to shoot free throws is very much like the acquisition of a skill. Everyone in the NBA is quite good at making baskets. But making them in a game is a performance of that skill, and it is usually much lower than the practice percentage. Why is this? The actual skill is the same, but the context is different. There are more people, more distractions, more pressure, more consequences, and more expectations during a game than in practice. It is the same for social interactions. Sometimes it can be harder to perform a social skill when it is not practice.

Social and emotional skills are no different. But remember no one is perfect. Interrupting someone can be easily fixed with a quick apology and then move on.

Remember from chapter 5 there is a difference between having symptoms and being impaired. Having a symptom like impulsivity and interrupting someone is not a big deal. Not caring and not doing anything about it can lead to a social impairment and not having friends. Knowing how ADHD affects you socially can help you make adjustments and be successful.

What Is a Self-Concept?

Self-concepts are the thoughts and feelings you have about yourself. Everything we do, every experience we have ever had, and every way we view the world adds to it. Self-concept is important because if it's good, we feel confident about and happy with ourselves. A positive self-concept is not about having a rose-colored view of yourself, like you are the best at everything all the time; this is not an accurate view of yourself or anything else. You also don't want to have a constant negative view of yourself, because this is not accurate either.

Having a good self-concept comes from liking the things about yourself that are good and being OK with the things you want to work on. No one is perfect. Maybe you are good at math or science or sports or music, or maybe you have great hobbies like watching movies or reading. Maybe there are things that you would like to work on, like making more friends or getting better grades. Having a good self-concept involves acknowledging the good and bad and accepting the things that can and cannot be changed. Having a good self-concept is about having an all-around positive view of yourself regardless of the things that you are good or bad at.

Try This

Try this exercise. Draw a circle in the middle of a piece of paper, write all of the things about yourself that you like inside the circle, and all of the things that you want to change outside the circle. Can you think of lots of things that you

Do you have an overall positive opinion of yourself? Does ADHD affect the way that you think about yourself? © iStock / MangoStar_Studio

like about yourself? Are the things that you would like to change, changeable? Is ADHD on the list? Do you put it on the inside or the outside of the circle? Do you have an overall positive view of yourself? Do you want to change things that cannot be changed? Do you accept that there are things that you can do and things that you can't do? Are you OK with this idea?

If you struggle with ADHD symptoms or have trouble in school, trouble making friends, or trouble with anything else, your self-concept might be affected. If you are working on improving yourself in these areas, don't be so hard on yourself. Remember social-emotional skills can be practiced, and no one is perfect.

What is your self-concept like? To find out, ask yourself questions such as the following:

- Do I consider myself damaged, disordered?
- Is there something wrong with me?
- Do I feel good about being me?
- What thoughts do I have about myself? Mostly good, mostly bad? Half and half? Are they accurate?
- Do I want to change things or make improvements?
- Do I want to change things that cannot be changed? Is that a useful way to think?

- Am I down on myself a lot?
- Are my expectations of myself, others, or life realistic?
- Am I unfairly judging myself by someone else's standards?

These types of questions can also be sorted out in counseling as we consider our self-concept.

According to ADHD author Dr. Ned Hallowell, "The real disability is shame, pessimism, negativity and no creative outlet."[2] Having a good self-concept can be like wearing a coat of armor that protects us from all of the negative events that can happen to us in our life.

In a TEDx talk about having ADHD, Angela Aquirre said,

It has been a long road to self-acceptance, I will tell you that, but the thing I want you all to leave here with today is not only a sense of compassion for people who are living with ADHD and other invisible disabilities it's the fact that my life has taken an unconventional but extraordinary path because of it. . . . And that is because I have learned that it is okay to be different, and more important it is okay to ask for help and accept it when you need it. The moment I began to embrace the part of who I am that makes me different instead of rejecting it is the moment I began to live my fullest life.[3]

An Invisible Disorder's Impact

There are some people who do not believe ADHD is real. Part of the reason for this may be that ADHD is not visible to some people. For example, people with ADHD do not use crutches, they do not have scars, they do not look different. This can add to your frustration if you have ADHD because others may not acknowledge your difficulties are real.

As one person with ADHD put it, "Because ADHD is not a visible disorder, people don't understand that it is just as disabling as those that are very visible. It requires understanding and acceptance that people with ADHD need some accommodations at times to perform to their potential."[4]

Disorders that are not visible can lead to difficulties. These difficulties can lead to negative thoughts and feelings that can affect your daily life, sometimes without you even knowing. For example, since ADHD is not visible, like someone using a wheelchair, people may not believe you have it. Maybe they will think that you are making excuses for your bad behavior. These types of thoughts may upset you. You may decide not to tell people that you have ADHD. Maybe you are scared people will find out. Maybe you feel like you have a secret. How about when you realize that ADHD is permanent? Maybe the thought will make you feel sad or angry. What if you do not live in an accepting environment? Perhaps you fear being stigmatized or being looked at as different. This can lead to worrying or anxiety. If you take medication or go to a psychologist will others find out and think you are crazy?

Everything that has been described here could be an unfortunate consequence of ADHD's invisibility. How does ADHD affect you emotionally? Here are some questions you can ask yourself:

- How do I feel about having ADHD?
- Do I feel different from other kids?
- Am I scared of people finding out I have ADHD?
- Do I feel like I will never be good at certain things?
- Am I scared of how people think of me having ADHD?

Getting the facts about ADHD can help. For example, if you feel different, it may help to know that right now, 6.4 million children are diagnosed with ADHD in the United States.[5] Do you still feel different? That is a lot of people. If you worry that you will never be good at anything, take a look at chapter 10 for a list of people with ADHD that are really good at lots of things. Sometimes others will still be mean and stigmatize. However, learning the facts can help you deal with the answers to your questions. Getting help from a knowledgeable person about ADHD can also help.

To Tell or Not to Tell

Since ADHD is not a visible disorder, people often find out you have it because you tell them. Before telling people that you have ADHD you may fear that they will see you differently or that you will be stigmatized or made fun of. The decision to tell people if you have ADHD is personal. So is telling others the details, such as whether you see a doctor or take medication or receive accommodations at school.

Sometimes you may choose to tell some people or not others depending on how close they are to you. You may choose to tell relatives, or close friends but not an acquaintance. Maybe you have to tell some people who work in a professional capacity, like the disability department at school, but not teachers. Maybe you will choose to share some information but not other information. These are all questions that you will end up asking and answering yourself at some point.

You can decide to tell people if you

- see a doctor
- take medication
- receive accommodations

You can also decide what information to share (if any) with

- immediate family
- extended family
- close friends
- teammates
- acquaintances
- people online
- doctors
- school personnel
- religious people

In deciding what to share and with whom, ask yourself the following questions:

- Who needs to know?
- Will they tell other people?
- For what purpose do they need to know?
- How does sharing this information help me?
- Are they trustworthy?
- Why am I sharing this information?

Sometimes people in professional capacities, like doctors, have rules about who they can share your information with; this is called confidentiality. But what about nonprofessionals or family members? What happens if someone finds out

"It's different now. I've no problem with people knowing that I have these issues or conditions or whatever you like to call them, because I'm an adult. But as a teenager, you know, you don't want to be judged or classified or be thought of as in some way defective, you know, so it was embarrassing."—an adult with ADHD[b]

Simone and Roxy

Olympic gold medalist Simone Biles's medical records were hacked, which resulted in the information about her having ADHD and taking medication being leaked to the public. She tweeted, "Having ADHD, and taking medicine for it is nothing to be ashamed of, nothing that I'm afraid to let people know."[c]

Formally diagnosed with ADHD as a teenager, Roxy Olin, of MTV's *The Hills* and *The City* fame, told *ADDitude* magazine, "I've learned, at this point in my life, that [ADHD] is a part of who I am. You don't have to keep your ADHD a secret."[d]

without your permission? Should you share things online where many people that you did not intend to know can learn about you? These are all questions that you may ask yourself before you share personal information.

Some people choose to talk openly about ADHD, some do not. Neither decision is right or wrong; the question is which is the right one for you. Some people have no problem letting other people know that they have ADHD, some like to keep it private. Sometimes when people get older and they have lived with ADHD for many years it is not a big deal to tell others. However, when they were younger they were not ready to tell people.

Sharing or not sharing is not a reflection of how comfortable you are with yourself. For example, you can choose not to share that you have ADHD and still be very proud of yourself. It does not mean you are ashamed. Much like toothpaste coming out of the tube, sometimes when it comes out you cannot put it back in, and if it doesn't help you in any way to share, then you may choose not to. Sometimes others' lack of understanding can lead to hurtful statements and bullying. On the other hand, after years of learning and dealing with ADHD, some use themselves as instruments to change how others think about ADHD by sharing their own story. The point is that there is no right or wrong way, only what works best for you.

Being stigmatized is a phrase that describes people seeing you in a negative way or disgraced for some reason. People who have differences are often stigmatized for lots of different reasons: the way they look, the way they act, or for having disabilities. Sometimes sharing your differences can help people who care about you have a greater understanding of who you are and the difficulties that you face. This can be a big help in life. Some people look at differences as a way to stigmatize, bully, and put down others. It may be helpful to talk to people that care about you or professionals with lots of experience to help make these decisions.

Think, Feel, Behave

Many psychologists believe that there is a direct link between how we think, feel, and behave. In other words the way we think affects the way we feel, and the way we feel affects the way we behave, and the way we behave affects the way we think, and so on. Having emotions is part of being human. It would not be accurate to say that we can always control our emotions and "choose how to feel"; however, this is not to say that we are powerless and do not have some input into how we think and feel about things.

Sometimes we have certain ways of thinking that are not accurate, do not get us what we want, and can make us overly upset. These ways of thinking are not only specific to ADHD. When we find ourselves thinking like this we can tell ourselves that it is not true and replace the thought with another way of thinking.

Common Bad Thinking Habits

Here's a list of common bad thinking habits that do not get us what we want:

- It's my way or the highway.
- That is horrible terrible or awful.
- I can't do anything right.
- I can't stand that.
- This always happens to me.
- I shouldn't have to deal with this.
- I deserve to have it, now.
- This is the worst day of my life.
- I shouldn't be treated like that; I deserve better.

As you read these thinking statements, can you picture how they may create strong emotions? They certainly do not sound like statements that we would say with a smile on our face, right? Saying things like this too often may make us have extreme feelings like anger, fear, or worry. You may ask, but what if those statements are true? Maybe they are, but getting overly upset about them will not help you. For example, as we learned in the schoolwork chapter a little test anxiety can help you stay focused but extreme anxiety will not help you take the test. Remember there are consequences to how you think and feel, and if those consequences do not help you they can be changed.

Alternative Ways of Thinking

Let's look at common negative thought patterns and alternative ways to approach the same situation.

Let's say you studied for a math test. You go to school the next day, ready to take the test. You get to the first question and you don't know the answer. You tell yourself,

> This is going to be bad, I'm going to totally fail this test. The first questions are usually the easiest, and I can't even get it right. I can't stand this. It always happens to me.

The emotional reactions to these statements are not going to be good, even if the statements are somewhat true. Statements like these will lead to panic or anger, and those feelings will not help you take the rest of the test.

What happens when we choose to say this instead:

> I was hoping to get the first question right but I don't know the answer. Its only one question. Let me skip it and go to the next question and try it. I studied for this test and I will go to a question I know.

Think how these statements will keep you in the game and help you take the rest of the test. In addition you might consider that everyone might get that question wrong or that it might be one of only a few you get wrong.

How about this example: You are walking down the hallway at school and see a few acquaintances talking that you would like to be friends with. You say to yourself,

> Oh, man, I'm getting nervous already. I am not going to bother talking to them, I don't have anything interesting to say anyway. Every time I try to talk to people I say something stupid. It always happens to me. If I were to talk to them and make an idiot out of myself, I would be so embarrassed. It would be awful and everyone would know that I am a boring person to talk to.

The emotional reactions to these statements are not going to be good either. Statements like these will lead you to be very anxious or perhaps not talk to them at all. You will end up not making any friends.

What happens when we choose to say this instead:

I am a little nervous about talking to these people. Maybe I can say hello and ask how they are doing. I don't have to be the best ever at talking to people to see how they are doing. If I don't know how to answer a question, it is not the end of the world. Everyone says the wrong thing sometimes; it could be a lot worse. Anyway, if they are that judgmental and don't want to be friends, I can find other people to be friends with.

These statements will make it much more likely to be successful talking to people, and you will be less nervous as well. Here are some other statements that you can say to yourself when you are having a tough time:

- I should collect all the facts before I come to conclusions.
- Although I would like it, I can't always have what I want.
- No one is perfect, including the person I am talking to.
- Not everything is my fault.
- Not everything is everyone else's fault.
- Some things are easy and some are hard; this one is hard.
- Not everything is such a big deal.
- Nothing is all good or all bad.
- This is not a big deal; it could be better but it could be much worse.
- Nothing is the end of the world.

Putting It Together

Let's put it all together. Social and emotional functioning can be affected by ADHD. It can affect our understanding of the way the world works and the expectations of others, ourselves, and our ability to meet those expectations. The way we look at and think about the world will affect our ability to successfully interact with it, as well as our emotional reactions to the world.

Having feelings is a good thing. Being able to express our feelings appropriately can be a great benefit to our lives. However, keeping feelings inside and not expressing them, or expressing them in a way that is not helpful, can have a negative effect on our lives. Remember knowing is half the battle.

TREATMENT

....

The following chapter is not meant to give advice or opinions or be a substitute for seeing a doctor and getting professional treatment. Rather this chapter is designed to help you understand the different types of treatment that there are available for ADHD. As discussed in previous chapters there is no cure for ADHD. In other words, it does not just go away, although some report their symptoms lessen with age. There are treatments you can do to make your life easier if you have ADHD. What we are talking about is what you can do to help yourself cope with ADHD. Treatment means going to a doctor or professional who can evaluate you, give his opinion, and help you decide what is the best way to treat your ADHD. Many times treatment involves some form of counseling, medication, or behavior training. Only a licensed professional can provide medical or psychological treatment for you.

People try many ways to cope with ADHD, including changes in diet, exercise, the amount of sensory stimuli one is exposed to, and many more. If something makes your life better, and does not harm you, then try it. If it works, then great. What medical and psychological professionals can do is to guide you in the right direction and let you know if something is healthy or not healthy for you. That decision is up to you and your doctor or mental health professional. There are many opinions about the best treatment for ADHD. What is true for some people is not true for others. This chapter provides you with information about who to talk to and what types of services they can provide.

When you are younger, the responsibility for treating your ADHD is primarily up to your parents or guardians. However, as you get older the responsibility to learn to live with ADHD is your own. You must learn to educate yourself and advocate for yourself. You must learn what you can do to help yourself. Did you know that in most places, when you are under the age of eighteen a doctor must get your parents' permission to give you treatment or even to speak with you? However, when you turn eighteen the doctor must have your permission to give you treatment or speak with you. Although laws differ from state to state, it is worth educating yourself about your own rights.

Confidentiality

Confidentiality is a term that you should know when you see your doctor, counselor, or therapist. Confidentiality means that when you tell your doctor something, she will not tell your parents or anyone else what you said. A medical doctor will not tell others about your health records. Sometimes, when you go to a doctor, this confidentiality agreement is part of the paperwork that you sign. Did you know that your conversations and health records with your doctor may be confidential? It is a question that you can ask. Specifically you can ask, "Will you tell my parents or anyone else the things that I tell you?" or "Are our conversations confidential?"[1]

There are different rules for confidentiality that depend on your age, the reason you are seeing the doctor, the place you see the professional (doctor's office or in school), and the specific laws in your state. There is a federal law to protect confidentiality, the Health Insurance Portability and Privacy Act (HIPPA). HIPPA is used in medical settings. The Family Education Rights and Privacy Act (FERPA) is used in school settings. There are also different state laws that determine the rules of confidentiality when you speak to a doctor, counselor, or therapist. A good way to find out about the confidentiality you have with your doctor is to ask.

Confidentiality can also be different from profession to profession. For example, confidentiality may be different when talking to a counselor or therapist than to a physician. In addition, depending on how old you are the rules of confidentiality may be different. A doctor may not have to keep her conversations with you confidential if you are under the age of eighteen. In this case she may tell your parents what you say or may choose not to. In some cases, a doctor may not tell your parents or anyone else the things that you say to her.

If you are using your parents' health insurance, they may receive statements that you have visited a doctor; however that does not mean the doctor can talk about why you went there or what you said. It is a conversation that you can have with your doctor.[2]

Although the rules from state to state differ, in many cases if you are at risk to be hurt, to hurt someone else, or to do something dangerous, a doctor may "disclose" what you have told him and tell someone else, including your parents. This is meant to keep you or someone else safe. As you get older, the conversation about confidentiality is a good conversation to have with your counselor, psychologist, or medical doctor. It can help to make you more comfortable sharing your thoughts, feelings, or challenges with them.

What Makes Something a Treatment?

People cope with the symptoms of ADHD in many different ways. Some target diet or exercise, some sensory input, and some social skills. There are many supports that people use to help them cope with their ADHD symptoms. Some people may join a gym, get a pet, or make new friends. Supports like these may not have been scientifically proven to reduce or help someone cope with ADHD symptoms, but that doesn't mean they don't work. Some supports that people use to cope with ADHD are really good health habits that anyone can use to make their life better, whether or not they have ADHD. Treatments are the types of services that a mental health or medical professional provide for you. What follows is a list of the most common treatments for ADHD and how they can be obtained.

Treatments for ADHD

According to the National Institute of Mental Health,[3] American Psychiatric Association,[4] Center for Disease Control,[5] and American Academy of Pediatrics,[6] the most common treatments for ADHD are medication, behavior training, and counseling.

- 43 percent of children with ADHD use medication alone
- 31 percent of children with ADHD receive a combination of medication and therapy
- 13 percent of children with ADHD receive behavior therapy only
- 13 percent of children with ADHD receive no treatment[7]

Many experiments and scientific studies have been performed around medication and therapy. There is proof, and a general agreement in the scientific community, that both medication and therapy help with the symptoms of ADHD.

Medication

Overall the most utilized treatment for ADHD is medication. Medications work by changing the chemistry in the brain to produce changes in behavior. Chapter 2 has information about the symptoms of ADHD. These symptoms include inattention, hyperactivity, and impulsivity. Medications that people usually take for ADHD help reduce these symptoms.

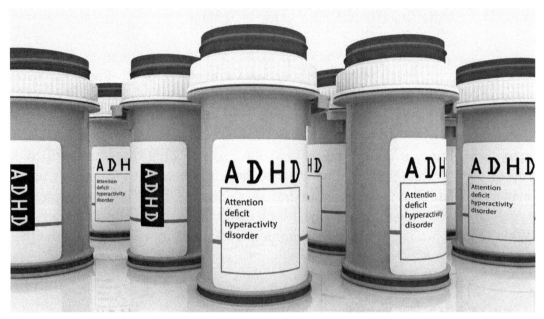

There are many different types of ADHD medications. Most ADHD medications fall under the category of stimulant. Medications can be obtained after an evaluation and diagnosis and can be prescribed by a medical doctor or professional who is licensed to prescribe medication. © iStock / mik38

Medication can only be prescribed by a medical doctor or professional who is licensed to prescribe medication, after you have received a diagnosis of ADHD. How do you know if medication is working? Medication works if it reduces one or some of the symptoms previously listed, making your life easier.

Medication can be a tough or personal decision for many. When children are young, the decision to take medication may be made by a parent. However, as you get older you will be more involved in the decision. Some people are in favor of medication, some are not, and some like medication when it works and do not when it doesn't. Dr. Ned Hallowell, a prominent author, speaker, and doctor on the topic of ADHD, stated that many people have asked him if he believes in Ritalin. He responded that he does not believe Ritalin is "a religious principle."[8] In other words, medication is not a belief system; it is a helpful tool that can be used if it works and discontinued if it doesn't. Everyone's brains are different and everyone's symptoms are different. That means that people respond to medication differently. For some medication may be the right decision, but not for others. It is important to communicate with your doctor if you are on medication or considering taking it for ADHD.

"The first time I took my medication it was like putting on glasses and realizing I could see without squinting, I could focus."—Jessica McCabe[a]

Side Effects

Some common side effects of stimulant medications:

- Decreased appetite
- Sleep problems
- Anxiety
- Irritability
- Stomachaches or headaches

Not everyone will experience these or any other side effects of medication. Some will experience other effects not listed. It is important to talk to your doctor about side effects.

Sometimes medications help to reduce symptoms of ADHD, but they can also have other effects. The side effects of different medications vary. You can have conversations and ask questions about the side effects of medication with your doctor. Sometimes people do not like the side effects of medications and they decide not to take them. Sometimes people may make a decision with their doctor to try a different medication because of side effects.

ADHD medications are generally referred to in two groups: stimulants and nonstimulants. Stimulant medications are referred to as a type of drug that stimulates the central nervous system. These medications generally help with the symptoms of ADHD. The FDA (Food and Drug Administration) has approved twenty-nine different stimulant medications in the United States. All the stimulant medications deliver one of two drugs: methylphenidate or amphetamine. Some medications are long lasting and some short.

Did You Know?

Many stimulant medications have both a drug name and a brand name. The *drug name* is the name for the chemical compound that makes up the medication. The *brand name* is a name that is given to the medication by the owners of the medication. For example, the drug acetaminophen is commonly referred to as Tylenol just like Ritalin is a common way to refer to methylphenidate.

Table 7.1 List of Commonly Used Stimulant Medications

Generic Name	Brand Name
Methylphenidate	AptensioXR, Concerta, Daytrana, Metadate CD, Methylphenidate HCl, MethylinTM, Quilichew ERTM, Quilivant XR, Ritalin, Ritalin LA, Ritalin SR
Dexmexylphenidate	Focalin, Focalin XR, Amphetamine Adzenys XR-ODT, Dyanavel XR
Dextroamphetamine	Dexadrine, Dexadrine ER, ProCentra, Zenzedi
Methamphetamine	Desoxyn
Mixed amphetamine salts	Adderall, Adderall XR
Amphetamine sulfate	Evekeo
Lisdexamfetamine	Vyvanase

Source: Drug Enforcement Administration (2016)

A word of caution: stimulant medications that contain methylphenidate or amphetamine are labeled controlled substances by the FDA,[9] which means they have a risk of misuse, abuse, and/or psychological or physical dependence.[10]

Other types of medications used to treat ADHD are nonstimulant medications. Non-stimulant medications are listed in table 7.2. All of the medications listed in the table are different and work differently than stimulant medications. They are not labeled controlled substances by the FDA, which means they do not run the risk for abuse, misuse, or physiological or psychological dependence.

Table 7.2 Nonstimulant Medications

Generic Name	Brand Name
Atomoxetine	Strattera
Clonidine	Kapvay
Guanfacine	Intuniv

Source: ADDitude *Magazine (2018).*

Behavior Training

Behavior training is generally meant for younger children with ADHD. Did you know that sometimes parents need help parenting? It's true; parents are not born having all the answers, especially about ADHD. Since children with ADHD sometimes have challenging behaviors, behavior training is a way of creating good behavioral habits in children. Behavior training is something that is used up until adolescence. Much of behavioral training involves giving rewards for good behaviors and sometimes punishments for negative behaviors.

Raising a child with ADHD can be challenging. For this reason many parents do not always know the best thing to do and the best way to deal with their own children. Just like you were not born knowing everything about ADHD, neither were your parents. Much like you are reading this book looking to learn more about ADHD, parents also benefit from education about ADHD. This is commonly referred to as parent training. This does not mean that parents are bad parents; it means they want to learn more about how to be great parents and how to deal with the special needs that someone with ADHD may have. Parent training can be from a knowledgeable mental health professional, school psychologist, or many other sources.

Did You Know?

Did you know that parent counseling and training is a service that is included on some individual education programs (IEPs)? It is meant to teach your parents skills to be better parents.

Therapy or Counseling

Therapy or counseling is a form of treatment for ADHD. The terms *counseling* and *therapy* differ in meaning from state to state. For our purpose we will define them as going to a licensed mental health professional to talk. When you get older, instead of your parents going to counseling, you may want to go to counseling or therapy.

So what is counseling or therapy? It can be very different from person to person. Counseling or therapy can involve talking. Some counselors or therapists will talk with you about your problems and try to help you find solutions. They can focus on your ADHD symptoms and try to help you get better at living life more effectively. Counselors and therapists can help you learn new behaviors that will allow you to manage your symptoms and reduce anxiety or increase your organization. Counselors and therapists can also can help you readjust the way that you look at life, teach and practice good social emotional skills with you, and help you to manage your emotions. Counseling and therapy can be for general issues that you may experience or very specific problems. Some counselors or therapists are trained and skilled at dealing with very specific problems that you may have, like if a family member passes away or you have been abused. Some even specialize in ADHD! Therapy or counseling can be a way for you to learn how ADHD affects your life and also what you can do to manage it.

So, wait. You may be wondering, "If I go to counseling, does that mean I am crazy?" Certainly not! Just like you go to a doctor for your physical health you

World Mental Health Day is on October 10th every year. It was first celebrated in 1992 and was started as a way to bring awareness to mental health issues and also to fight the stigma of mental health. Get more info at www.who.int/mental_health/world-mental-health-day/en/. © *iStock / InfiniteGraphic*

can go to a counselor or therapist for your mental health. Counseling and therapy can help you take care of your own mental health. Counseling can involve talking, playing, doing arts and crafts, or learning. In school, counseling can be in the form of a small group or one on one. Small-group counseling can help you develop better social skills and make friends with others.

Counseling or therapy is something that can be performed by a mental health professional, including a psychologist, psychiatrist, mental health counselor, social worker, and others. Counseling is something that you can get in school as part of your IEP or outside of school by a mental health provider. Counseling can be paid for by you or your parents insurance if it is outside the school. Some social working agencies provide counseling services.

In conclusion, the main treatments for ADHD are therapy, medication, or a combination of the two. Getting treatment for ADHD starts with going to your medical doctor or psychologist. There is nothing wrong with asking for help and trying to learn more about what to do if you have ADHD.

Questions and Answers

Aren't Kids Overmedicated in the United States?

It depends on who you ask. Remember: in order to receive medication, you must get evaluated, receive a diagnosis, and then be prescribed medication. Everyone's opinion is different about how easy it is to obtain a diagnosis and medication. If a trusted adult or doctor thinks you should be evaluated, it may be worth looking into.

Will Medications Mess Up My Brain Forever?

There is no proof that taking medication for ADHD has long-term negative side effects. Medications such as stimulants used to treat ADHD are only in your body for a short time before they are gone.

If I Take Medication, Doesn't That Mean I Am Too Weak to Just Pay Attention on My Own?

Absolutely not! If medication helps with your symptoms, great! Remember: ADHD is not a disorder of not trying hard enough or being lazy. Maybe you can focus for short periods, but you need to focus for longer periods, especially in school. There is nothing lazy about wanting to work for longer periods of time.

Doesn't Going to a Therapist or Counselor Make Me Crazy?

Definitely not. Seeing a therapist or counselor does not make you crazy. It means that you would like to work on mental health issues. This makes you confident and willing to improve yourself. Would you tell someone going to college that they would like to learn more because they are stupid? Of course not. They would like to go to school to better themselves. It is the same with going to counseling.

Can Anything I Say in Counseling Be Used against Me by My Parents and School?

Having a conversation about confidentiality with your doctors is important. Learning about what they can share and what they cannot share can help you feel more open and honest about the problems that you are having.

HOME LIFE
AND FAMILY

The relationships that you have with family members can be the most important relationships that you will have in life. It is important to know that ADHD can have a big impact on them. Let's first look at statistics about families in the United States:

- 73.7 million children are under the age of eighteen
- 69 percent of children live with two parents
- 23 percent of children live with a single mother
- 4 percent live with a single father
- 4 percent live with no parent
- Average size of a household is 2.5 people
- Divorce rate in the United States is between 33 percent and 45 percent

There were over 37 million households in the United States with children:

- 15 million had one child
- 13 million had two children
- 5 million had three children
- 2 million had four or more children[1,2]

Some facts about siblings in the United States:

- 82.22 percent of youth eighteen and under lived with at least one sibling
- More than 10 percent of households with children included step or adoptive siblings[3]

Within this data there can be any number of other combinations of families that are multicultural, have multiple generations living together, speak more than one language, are divorced, or live in blended households. This means infinite combinations of family structures can exist, successfully or unsuccessfully, before we even begin to think about ADHD.

Heritability

Did you know that ADHD could run in families?[4] It's true, although scientists do not totally agree on how inheritable it is. Some estimates state that if one of your parents has ADHD you have a 20–40 percent chance of having it.[5] This is compared to the rest of the population, which has a 5 percent chance.[6] That means that if one of your parents has ADHD, you are six times more likely than the rest of the population to have ADHD. If both of your parents have it, then your chances of having ADHD are even higher. There have been many studies completed on twins with ADHD. Those studies have found that if one twin has ADHD, the other twin has an 80 percent chance of having it.[7] That is a huge number and shows that ADHD is at least partly inheritable. It can be passed on, and if you have it there is a strong possibility someone else in your family has it.

Studying twins is one of the ways that scientists link ADHD to genetics. © iStock / strickke

"I was so reluctant to try meds for my son. I thought it would sedate him, make him a zombie and stifle his creativity. But I got to a point where I felt his ADHD would destroy our family, and we turned to medication. It turned out to be a wonderful decision. His grades turned around completely (top of his class), and he began to feel intelligent and capable. He could focus enough to express his fabulous ideas. Soon, we realized his dad also suffered from ADHD. We got him on meds too, and it's been a life changer for our whole family dynamic. Dad feels bitter about not getting the meds as a child, and feels he could have done more in life (it's not too late!). So I want people to know that just as someone with bad eyesight needs glasses, ADHD medication can allow you to reach your potential."—parent of a child and wife of husband with ADHD[a]

Parents

Knowing that ADHD is inheritable is not the only important piece of information that you need to know. *Newsflash!* Parents are not perfect. What if your parents have ADHD? Do you think this would make your life easier or harder? It is important to realize that if your parents have ADHD they may have some of the same struggles that you have. Maybe your parents never learned some of the material in this book, or never fully learned to cope with having ADHD. This can make family life more difficult. If your parents have not totally mastered ADHD, they may have a harder time helping you. Maybe a parent does not have ADHD, and she has no idea what it is like to have ADHD and what you are going through. This could be even worse, because she may fall victim to some of the same incorrect thinking that others have like you are lazy or a troublemaker.

Having a child with ADHD is not always easy. Sometimes parents do not have all of the answers. Sometimes parents get frustrated and need help as well. Maybe you are having trouble in school or making friends. Your troubles can have an effect on your parents. There is one thing for certain: if you are having a hard time because of ADHD, then your family members are also having a hard time because they love and care for you. Research suggests that parents with kids that have ADHD are more likely to have difficulty parenting because of it.

Maybe you are getting in trouble in school and your parents are punishing you. This can lead to difficulties in families, anger at parents, and also parents feeling bad because of it. I don't think any parent wakes up every day and says to himself,

> "'I don't have too much time so PAY ATTENTION, WHATS WRONG WITH YOU! FOCUS, for someone so smart you can be so stupid, I mean how could you forget about that we just talked about it. CUDDY something wrong with yo brain, do even think?' One thing I forgot to mention is that all of the expressions that I began with have something in common, they have all been said to me by people who have proven time and again their unconditional love, support, and willingness to do anything for me but in those moments they were extremely frustrated."—Salif Mahamane, a PhD student with ADHD[b]

"Gee, I think I would really like to get in an argument with my daughter today and punish her. That would just make a great day." If you are having trouble with your parents or have gotten into some bad habits like getting overly angry or arguing, think about going to your school counselor for advice about what to do.

Siblings

Perhaps your brother or sister has ADHD; perhaps neither does. Remember: you have a higher chance of having ADHD if one of your siblings does. It has been reported that having ADHD can have some negative impacts on your relationships with your brothers or sisters, for example:

- Aggression toward your brother or sister
- Parents asking you brother or sister to take care of you
- Unfair treatment

Aggression toward Your Brother or Sister

It is normal for siblings to have disagreements at times; however it is important how you disagree. You may want to ask yourself if you find yourself doing the following:

- Often disagreeing with siblings
- Always taking the opposite point of view
- Arguing or being nasty with others
- Being physically aggressive with your siblings

⚠ Learn to Judge Your Reactions

● Learn to judge whether you are overreacting or having emotional reactions that are much more intense than needed. Do you find yourself reacting emotionally very quickly and intensely? This may not be a helpful way to behave.

- Being verbally aggressive with your siblings
- Trying to control what your siblings do
- Being manipulative

The question is, "Are you the bully?" and "Are you victimizing your brother or sister?" These are all bad habits and can have negative effects on your siblings or anyone else. Disagreements are not always so easy or one sided—your brother or sister may not be so nice to you sometimes—but if you find yourself getting into these patterns of behavior, you may be having a negative impact on your sibling. That is the bad news. The good news is that these are behaviors and you can change them. Remember if you want to change behaviors, you can always seek treatment by a professional to help you change how you think, feel, or act.

Parents Asking Your Brother or Sister to Take Care of You

ADHD can also affect your relationship with your sibling if your parents are asking him to take care of you. Brothers and sisters helping each other is a good thing. Brothers and sisters are meant to look out for one another, but teaching and protecting children is the job of the parent, not a brother or sister. If a parent is asking a brother or sister to do a parent job, it is not appropriate. Just like a parent should not ask you to go out and go to work to pay the bills, she should not ask you or your sibling to take care of each other. This is a grown-up responsibility, not a kid's. Here are some quotes from siblings of children with ADHD:

- "I took on the motherly role and disciplined my brother. I was always the disciplinarian with him, even now."
- "I was the one who took care of things. I was the one who gave her medicine."
- "At first I was a little bit annoyed and irritated about it because now I had more responsibility, making sure that she is taking her tablets and stuff like that. And I also helped her with her homework and stuff so, whenever we had to do the homework and helping out with stuff it just took hours."

- "I had an obligation to look after my ADHD sibling and do what the parent could not. I had to take her to her room and take care of her in order to protect my sister from the violence in the home."[8]

Brothers and sisters should not have grown-up responsibilities because this situation can lead to problems between siblings, including resentment. A kid's job is to be a kid, not a parent. It is important to realize that this situation is not the fault of either sibling—the one with or without ADHD—but rather the parents who asked a brother or sister to act like a parent.

Unfair Treatment

The third way ADHD can affect your siblings is that they believe that they are treated unfairly. Maybe your parents have one expectation for you and another for your brother or sister. For example, you have to pass a class, but your brother or sister is expected to get an A. Or maybe a phone call home for poor behavior in school is expected for you, but for your brother or sister it would result in a huge punishment. These situations might cause your brother or sister to say, "That's not fair. If I did that I would get in big trouble." These feelings can lead to resentment.

Siblings might also feel jealous because more attention is paid to you because of your behaviors. Some siblings of kids with ADHD have made the following comments:[9]

- "He got more attention."
- "Everything revolved around my brother and it almost was like it had to go his *way.*"
- "There were times when we were shopping for stuff for me and if my brother got tired or bored they would have to go home. This made me feel jealous in a way and cheated out of a lot of things because he had ADHD and I didn't. It was unfair to me."
- "He had four different tutors, one for each subject, but I had none."

Some might describe this as the squeaky wheel getting the oil, but it can leave brothers and sisters feeling bad. This could also leave some siblings feeling sad, angry, or bitter, as shown in the following sibling comments:[10]

- "Just go help your son; he needs you more than me."
- "I would just go and hide and cry and stuff. I remember there was this one little cupboard on the floor in my mom's room that did not have anything in it. This used to be my crying spot. So I would just go and retreat in there."

Siblings might also feel angry over differences in discipline:[11]

- "When I was in Grade 1, I had to do a minimum of an hour of homework every day and even if I did not have homework to do my parents made stuff for me to complete. My brother, on the other hand, would finish only half of the required work and when he did not want to do anymore mom or dad would do the rest for him."
- "They are more lenient with her and when she performs or has a tantrum because they are disciplining her, they just take away the discipline and the threats."

Many siblings feel they are part of family system that didn't work for them but rather for their brother or sister. This situation may hinder the non-ADHD individual's development as well because he or she does not always get what is needed. If a family is not working harmoniously and peacefully, it can leave your brother or sister feeling sad or wishing for a normal family.

ADHD can affect families in many ways. However, families may have problems in addition to ADHD that can make life difficult. © *iStock / macrovector*

You

How can having ADHD affect you in your family life? In many ways. It is possible that you have a great relationship with your siblings and parents, that you do not fight, argue, or have disagreements. Great! However, maybe the opposite is true; you get in trouble with your parents, have a tough time getting along with your siblings, or are always being compared to your brother or sister. Maybe you have been labeled the troublemaker in the family and have a reputation. Maybe you think you are the least favorite child. These are all ways that ADHD *can* affect your family life but remember: things can get better. Knowing is half of the battle. Maybe it is a relief for you to know that some of the problems you have in your family are due to ADHD and not because you are a bad person. Maybe reading this chapter will give you a new outlook toward your siblings and motivate you to treat them better.

What Do I Do If My Family Life Is Really Bad?

If your family life is not pleasant, the first thing you can do is talk to your counselor at school. Depending on the rules from state to state you can meet with your school counselor at least one time without having to inform your parents. He can be a good resource to guide you in the right direction.

Family Harmony

All families are different. Maybe you come from a large family with lots of brothers and sisters, aunts, uncles, and cousins. Maybe you come from a smaller family that is just the members of your immediate household. Maybe you come from a family where your parents are divorced. Maybe you do not have any brothers or sisters. Families come in all shapes and sizes and there is no one right way to have a "good family." Families are about relationships and good relationships make good families. Did you know that family harmony is a protective factor against mental illness and also substance abuse?[12] Having a happy family life is not some concept from a TV sitcom. It is something that can seriously affect your health and well-being for the rest of your life.

As a family unit, anything that affects your brother or sister or mother or father also affects you! If your brother or sister or mother or father has a bad day, their bad day will also affect you in some way. It is an important lesson to learn

"ADHD is a neurological and behavioral disorder that affects not only the person with it, but the entire family, including parents and the extended family of parental siblings and grandparents. It tests the limits of the family's ability to be supportive, understanding, and loving."—parent of a child with ADHD[c]

because once you realize the impact your family has on you—and the impact you have on them—you may think twice before you interact negatively with them.[13]

Families also have their own social rules, like the way they talk to one another, how they argue or joke around, and how parents discipline. They also have their own traditions and daily routines, like celebrating special occasions and having family meals. Social rules, traditions, and daily routines all contribute to the family unit and how well the family functions.

In addition, families can have problems that have nothing to do with ADHD. There are also outside influences on a family. Parents may have a demanding work schedule. Maybe your family is having financial difficulties. Maybe certain family members have health problems. Maybe your parents are exhausted and do not have time for you, or they are not getting along with one another. All of these problems can affect how happy or stress-free family life is.

One last family trait to think about is your schedule. People with ADHD function much better in a predictable environment with a schedule and balance. It is a lesson that you may learn for yourself when you go to college. Knowing when meal times are, having clean laundry, and keeping your living space organized are important for you to be successful. We discussed this in one way or another in other chapters. For example, your backpack and desk should be organized in school to be successful, your dorm room in college and your room at home as well. Predictable interactions with your family and predictable interactions with your environment can be the difference between success and failure.

Many times families that are running well are predictable. I don't think anyone wants to come home every night wondering what they will find when they go through the front door. This type of excitement is unwanted and leads to emotional instability and chaos. Do what you can to stay on a predictable schedule, keep your room clean, do your chores, and maintain positive interactions with your family members. At the same time, however, remember that the overall social, emotional, and financial managing of the family is not your job. It's the job of an adult—your parents.

In conclusion, when untreated and unrecognized, ADHD can have a negative impact on a family. When the proper supports are in place a person with ADHD can be a positive addition to a family.

ADHD SUPERPOWERS

....

*"People are like bicycles. They can keep their balance only
as long as they keep moving."—Albert Einstein*

Viewing the symptoms of ADHD as all bad is a matter of perspective. As the expression goes, no matter how flat the pancake, it still has two sides. ADHD is no different. Whether ADHD is a gift or a curse has been a matter of debate. Drs. Ned Hallowell and Russell Barkley, prominent in the field of ADHD research, have discussed this topic. They came to a conclusion. ADHD is neither a gift nor a curse.[1]

Of course there are difficulties associated with ADHD, but people with ADHD have strengths as well. In order to understand the strengths of ADHD, we have to change our perspective. What really makes something a disorder? In order to have a disorder one must have symptoms. Examples of ADHD symptoms are impulsivity, distractibility, and hyperactivity—maybe you cannot pay attention in class, or you call out when the teacher is teaching, or you do not do your homework, or you break school rules. However, the symptoms alone are not enough to qualify as a disorder. The symptoms must cause impairments in major life activities. We can think of impairments as the consequences of our symptoms. Impairments prevent us from performing important life activities. Getting failing grades and being suspended are impairments in school.

But imagine if you went to a school that that did not grade; you would not have failing grades. What if there was no homework? You would not get in trouble for not handing it in. What if all the classes were like science labs where you had to talk and converse with partners in order to complete the experiment? You would not get in trouble for having to remain silent for an entire period. Unfortunately, most schools do not work like this (but maybe they should). In a school like this, you would still have ADHD symptoms, but there would be no impairment. In other words, the environment plays a role in symptoms and impairments.

When we are young, going to school is not a choice. However, as we get older we have a lot more to say about our major life activities. For example, we can choose what we do for a living, who our friends are, what we study in school, where we go to school, and so on. In other words, we can create our own environment.

What if we changed the way we thought about the symptoms of ADHD? What if we could make positives out of them? According to psychiatrist Ned Hallowell we can take the ADHD symptoms that would usually cause impairments and turn them on their head to create what he calls ADHD mirror traits. For example, distractibility turned on its head is like curiosity. Impulsivity turned on its head is like creativity. Hyperactivity turned on its head can be thought of as having a lot of energy.[2]

Thinking about ADHD in this way is not meant to downplay the struggles that people with ADHD have in life. It is meant to illustrate two points: First, we all have a choice in how we view ourselves. Although there may be struggles in life, we do not have to think of ourselves as damaged or disordered. A realistic view of life is that there are positives and negatives associated with any situation. Second, we can strive to create an environment that fosters and rewards our special gifts instead of punishing us for them. In chapter 10, we will look at some individuals who have been very successful at using their ADHD superpowers to their advantage. In this chapter, we will look at the ADHD superpowers of imagination, creativity, curiosity, hyperfocus, neurodiversity, energy, sense of humor, and helping others.

Imagination

Albert Einstein stated that "imagination is more important than knowledge. Knowledge is limited while imagination encircles the world."[3] Imagination is the act of forming new ideas or fantasies or creating novel thoughts with our mind. People with ADHD can be very imaginative. Imagination is a process of looking at things from a different perspective and is a major contributor to creativity. According to some researchers, people with ADHD have more brain activity in the "imagination network" of their brain.[4]

The imagination network is involved in "constructing dynamic mental simulations based on personal past experiences such as used during remembering, thinking about the future, and generally when imagining alternative perspectives and scenarios to the present." The imagination network is also involved in social cognition, for instance, imagining what someone else is thinking.[5]

Imagination is active when you are thinking of ways to solve problems or practice in your mind what you would do in a situation. It is also active when you are daydreaming, or thinking "What if?" or "What would you rather do?" Imagination can be a great source of enjoyment and instrumental in problem solving.

According to Salif Mahamane, a doctoral student with ADHD, "Brainstorming, sure my mind is rarely quiet but I am comfortable in that. The sheer number of thoughts and ideas is astounding. Even if a lot of them are bad or half-baked they are great jumping off points for deeper thinking. One distraction can lead to an unending train of thought fueled by intrigue for each next thing, it's like popping popcorn, one kernel goes and then they all take off."[6]

Creativity

Imagination is important for creativity. If we think of imagination as the idea, then creativity is how to apply that idea in real life. We use imagination and creativity all the time in our everyday life. Creativity is the number one ADHD superpower; it is a very special trait that people with ADHD have. How do we know someone is creative? Good question. If someone is smart, he may receive a high score on a test. If someone is funny, she will make us laugh. If someone is strong, he can lift a lot of weight. But what if someone is creative?

The answer is not so easy. Artists are creative—maybe they can write a poem or a song—but not all creative people are artists. There is no absolute way we can measure creativity, but there are tests associated with creativity. Usually when we test someone, whether it be an IQ test, reading test, or math test, it is easy: we are testing someone's ability to give the right answer. Tests of creativity are a little different, though. Often tests of creativity do not have a right answer. Being creative is all about finding answers that no one has thought of yet. How do you score a test if there are no right answers? How do we know if someone is creative then? Scientists use the term *divergent thinking* to explain creative thought. Divergent thought explains a way of thinking that allows someone to come up with multiple solutions to a problem. People with ADHD have higher scores on tests of divergent thinking.

Here is an example of divergent thinking from the classic comedy movie *Airplane!* In one scene, a weather report is handed to the head air traffic controller. After looking at the report for a few seconds, he hands the paper to one of the other air traffic controllers and says, "Johnny, what can you make of this?" Johnny looks at the paper for a moment and then puts it on his head and says, "I can make a hat"; then he puts it on his chest and says, "or a broache"; and then waves it in the air and says, "or a pterodactyl." Of course, these were not the answers the air traffic controller wanted to hear, and he immediately took the paper back.[7]

Johnny's answer is truly the essence of what cognitive neuroscientists and psychologists call divergent thinking: he gave multiple outside-of-the-box answers to the same question.

Some tests that are commonly used by researchers to measure creativity are based on the ability to find uncommon or different uses for items just like Johnny did in the movie. An example of this is a droodle test. A droodle is a picture of something that is actually nothing. "Droodle tests are great measures of divergent thinking," describes Scott Barry Kaufmann, a cognitive neuroscientist at the University of Pennsylvania. Droodle tests involve looking at objects that have no real meaning and making up your own. The idea behind a droodle is to name as many uses for the object or possibilities for what the object is in a short period of time. People who name more uses are considered to be thinking divergently or creatively. When looking at a droodle, you cannot rely on your current understanding of the object because it has no real meaning. You must think outside the box. People with ADHD tend to score higher on tasks of divergent thinking because they require creativity.

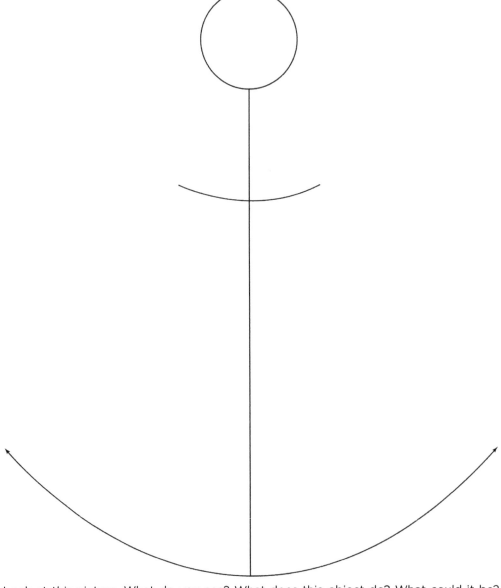

Look at this picture. What do you see? What does this object do? What could it be? Think of as many answers as you can. Use your imagination. © *iStock / Birgul Zalkhayeva*

Aaron Bruno

In an interview, singer-songwriter Aaron Bruno from Awolnation was asked about a line from his hit song "Sail" that says "Blame it on my ADD." He responded, "I was told I had ADD around the age of 15, and I was confused at first, but then just accepted it as a gift and moved on. That's what I tell people who ask about it." He stated that "sometimes if we simply admit and look at our problems and struggles straight in the face, other people can relate and possibly do the same in their own way." Referring to the song, he said, "These ideas come to my head out of nowhere and I do my best to turn them into musical realities."[a]

Look at the image on page 120. What do you see? Maybe you see a mouth and nose, or a smiley face, or an anchor, or a fishing hook, or a boy standing in the middle of a seesaw, a doorknocker, or a scarecrow. The sky is the limit when it comes to creativity and imagination. Did you know that children are better at droodle tests than adults? It seems somewhere along the way we lose our ability to be silly and think creatively.

Creativity is not only the ability to come up with multiple answers, but also the ability to determine which answers would be of some use in real life. Then you can create something. That means creativity is not only a gift that is useful for artists. Creative thinkers can solve real-life problems. For example, people who are creative often find more solutions to problems. This is often referred to as *thinking outside the box*. Also creativity can allow people to solve problems that others thought were impossible or even to see problems that no one knew existed.

Research supports the notion that people with ADHD characteristics are *more likely* to reach higher levels of creative thought and achievement than people without these characteristics. Both creative thinkers and people with ADHD show difficulty suppressing brain activity coming from the "imagination network."[8]

In his TEDx talk, Theo Siggelaki explains how a game called the Wikipedia game illustrates how his creative mind works differently than others':

When we would get bored in class we would play this game and the way it worked is that you pick one page, and then you pick a really random second page, and whoever could get to the really random second page first would win. I always won. So today we are going to play the Wikipedia game just to see how my mind works. We are going to start with Kenneth Starr and we will get to Gibson guitars. I don't know if you remember Kenneth Starr, he investigated Clinton in the 90s. Anyway, so we are going to be on Mr. Starr's page, we are going to pick a nice broad topic: America (click on it); this takes us to the United States page, on that page we are going to go to the culture section, we are going to click on Chuck Berry . . . there's Chuck, he happens to be playing a Gibson guitar. And in four clicks we made it to Gibson, two seemingly random topics transitioned fluidly in four clicks, that is how my brain works.[9]

Curiosity

There is not a lot of research on curiosity and the term itself isn't really defined, which makes it a hard thing to study. Some people call it motivation; some call it novelty-seeking behavior. Lack of curiosity has been linked to depression, and too much curiosity has been linked to distractibility and ADHD. Research on curiosity is closely related to ADHD because people who have ADHD have a harder time inhibiting their responses to new stimuli.

However, the anecdotal evidence that people with ADHD are curious is substantial. Curiosity can be defined as the drive for information. What interests you? What do you find interesting? If you have ADHD, you might be interested in many things and be more curious than others. Maybe you have the need to know what something is, or how it works. It is fun to know why something works. Every time you click on a story on the Internet or look at something or make an experiment to see how it works, you are being curious. What is the difference between someone who is curious and someone who is simply distractible? Environment is the key. If you are so curious that you never accomplish anything, you are distractible. If your curiosity is harnessed and it allows you to problem solve, it is a great gift.

Many people who know someone with ADHD would swear that they are always noticing things: differences, new things, shiny things, stuff that is moving. It may be something that has changed in a room, something new, something missing; they may even have a sixth sense. There could be a neurological reason for this. When neuroscientists test attention, sometimes they use tasks that require us to inhibit our responses. *Inhibit* is a big word to say *ignore.*

Sometimes, as when we're studying, we choose to ignore sounds—the sound of cars passing by or the sound of someone cooking in the kitchen—but sometimes our brains ignore things without us even knowing it. Think about it. Ignoring differences or novel stimuli can make it easier for us to do things. Some people are better than others at ignoring things. However, in some tasks people with ADHD brains overreact to novel stimuli, their brains simply cannot ignore them, whether they want to or not. What this distractibility means is that people with ADHD notice things that other people's brains block responses to.

This is the basis for the thought that people with ADHD are curious: they simply cannot ignore new things. They want to know what it is, why it is there, and what it does. Is being overly curious a bad thing? Again, it depends on the context. If you work in a dynamite factory, maybe being overly curious is not such a great quality; however, if you are a detective, artist, or scientist it can be quite a valuable trait. Curiosity is linked to people who love learning and are motivated to learn.

Hyperfocus

A developing area in ADHD research is the idea of hyperfocus. Hyperfocus is a phenomenon that has been observed in people with ADHD. This is the ability to be incredibly engaged in an activity for an extended period of time. Hyperfocus has been compared to the idea of *flow* in psychology that was proposed by Hungarian psychologist Mihály Csíkszentmihályi.

Some people refer to the mental state of flow as being in "the zone." Flow is the mental state in which a person performing an activity is fully immersed in a feeling of energized focus, full involvement, and enjoyment in the process of the activity. There are seven characteristics of flow:

1. Being completely involved in what you are doing
2. Having a sense of being outside everyday reality
3. Having a great sense of inner clarity
4. Knowing that the activity is doable
5. Having a sense of calmness
6. Losing sense of time
7. Having intrinsic motivation[10]

In essence, flow is characterized by complete absorption in what one does, to the point of losing sense of space and time. Dr. Ned Hallowell, psychiatrist and author of many books including *Driven to Distraction*, explains that people with ADHD can often experience a flow-like state when they are immersed in an activity. Two key ingredients of flow are being goal directed and calm, which does not include hours of mindless activity.

How can people with ADHD engage in a flow-like state if they cannot sustain attention? This question makes more sense if we look at ADHD as a problem focusing attention, not only sustaining it. Imagine a camera with an autofocus that is not working properly: sometimes it is focused and sometimes everything is blurry. It is not the lens that is broken but the system that regulates the focus of the lens. At times people with ADHD pay attention to everything, and at other times they hyperfocus on only one thing. It is debatable whether *flow* and *hyperfocus* are

"One trait is hyperfocus. When I'm interested in something I can give it 150 percent. The rest of the world is stuck at 100."—Theo Siggelakis[b]

comparable, but the fact that people with ADHD exhibit long uninterrupted periods of concentration has been well documented. Many people that write about ADHD see hyperfocus as an advantage.

Neurodiversity

Why are some people creative and some not? Why do some people have ADHD and some don't? It is a good question. If ADHD is all bad, why do people still have it? According to evolutionary theories like natural selection, if the traits that are associated with ADHD are bad traits, wouldn't they have been unselected over the years? Or at least they would not be increasing. Some genetic researchers investigate genetic markers for ADHD and have suggested that genes linked with ADHD have been positively selected throughout human history.[11]

Neurodiversity theories are about the belief that diversity is good for humans and provides an advantage.[12] This diversity is linked to genetic variation and the fact that advantages and disadvantages humans have can only be looked at in context.[13] This means the individual symptoms of ADHD can be beneficial if they are put into the right situation. Other researchers have hypothesized that ADHD-like traits could have been advantageous over the course of human history, but more research needs to be done to support these theories.[14]

Genetic research done among African tribes split into hunter-gatherers and farmers found that people who had genetic disposition for ADHD were better nourished when they lived with the hunter-gatherers. The researcher found that the people who were genetically predisposed to ADHD and lived with the farmers were less nourished. This has led some to believe that there may have been genetic advantages to the predisposition of ADHD in nomadic hunter-gathers.[15]

Scholars have suggested that when indigenous people migrated from Asia to North America, some settled in the north and some kept migrating south. Some scientists also say it is possible that because of ADHD genetic markers, those individuals who kept moving south may have been better suited for the nomadic demands and traveling. This might explain why today there is a higher percentage of individuals with genetic markers associated with ADHD in the southern part of North America compared to the north. These final points are a matter of controversy and debate. However, there is a general agreement in the scientific community that a certain amount of genetic diversity is important for the survival of any race.

Energy

The *Diagnostic and Statistical Manual*, fifth edition, lists some of the symptoms of ADHD as being driven by a motor and being extremely talkative. In addition individuals with ADHD leave their seats when they should be sitting and also run, dash, or climb when it is not appropriate. In fact if we look at these symptoms of ADHD—more activity, driven by a motor—we will start to see a trend. This is the description of someone who is energetic.

It is debatable whether being hyperactive is comparable to or the same as having lots of energy, but one thing is for sure: people who are hyperactive move a lot. At the beginning of the chapter we pointed out there are environments where moving around a lot and being talkative would be a plus. If you can be in an environment like that, being hyperactive would be positive and not a negative.

For example, if you love books and have ADHD you may not want to consider working in a library where you would have to be quiet, not talk for extended periods, and be slow and deliberate in your movements as you stock the shelves. Hyperactivity and being talkative would not be considered superpowers in a library. If you love books *and* like to talk and move around, maybe owning a bookstore would be more your speed: you would perform basically the same duties as a librarian but you would have to stock the shelves quickly, be able to talk to lots of people to sell books, move around, and make the rules in your store. This example is meant to illustrate that there is nothing that you cannot do but lots of things you may not want to do. What is a superpower in the bookstore would be considered kryptonite in the library.

Sense of Humor

Divergent thinking is finding multiple answers to the same question, so what is humor? Well it's kind of the same thing, only it's finding ridiculous answers to the same question. Think back to our droodle test; maybe you thought of a funny reason that the man was jump roping in a box. People who are able to think divergently are linked to creativity. Similarly, creativity is linked to sense of humor. It would be overly simplistic to say that people with ADHD are all funny or have a great sense of humor, but there is evidence that divergent thinkers have a good sense of humor and people with ADHD fit into this description.[16] Just perform a Google search on *ADHD and comedians* and see what comes up.

There is no formal research that there are a higher number of comedians with ADHD, but numerous comedians talk about it. Comedian Sinbad discussed being diagnosed with ADHD. He described performing two-and-a-half-hour comedy shows, while keeping the audience engaged. He said, "I have ADHD, it's a gift, if you pick the right job it's a gift."[17] Comedian Rory Bremner talks about the difficulties growing up with ADHD and being "very scatty as a young child." His classmates would laugh at him, which he jokingly said "was an advantage if you were a comedian."[18]

Comedian and comedy writer Rick Green has started a website called TotallyADD.com with many personal accounts and blogs about having ADHD. He also wrote and directed a documentary called *ADD and Loving It* starring fellow comedian Patrick McKenna, who received an ADHD diagnosis. Comedian and *America's Got Talent* judge Howie Mandel also talked about having ADHD and OCD (obsessive-compulsive disorder) as a child and knowing he was different. In addition, comedians Jeff Allen and Allen Goodwin both use their own ADHD as material in their comedy routines. Comedian Jeff Nichols has also said he has ADHD,[19] and Vince Vaughan stated in an interview that he was diagnosed with ADHD and dyslexia in school. Other comedians have been suspected of having ADHD and many other entertainers may not have a formal diagnosis. There may be no formal link between ADHD and comedy, but there are a lot of comedians with ADHD and they are funny.

Helping Others

> One day a girl is walking down the street when she falls into a manhole and cannot get out. A doctor passes by and the girl shouts up, "Hey Doc. Can you help me out?" The doctor writes a prescription, drops it down in the hole, and moves on. Along walks a judge and she shouts up, "Hey, your honor, can you help me out?" The judge writes out an order, drops it down in the hole, and moves on. Finally, a friend walks by and the girl shouts up, "Hey, can you help me out of this hole?" Her friend jumps in the hole and the girl says, "Why did you do that? Now we are both stuck down here." Her friend says, "Yes, but I have been down here before and I know how to get out."[20]

This story is the essence of peer mentoring: someone who has been in a situation before helping out another person who is in the same situation. Maybe you have been the person who has needed help or maybe you are in a position to help someone else. Mentoring is the last superpower. Mentoring is not only limited to ADHD but can be found in many different professions and walks of life. Mentoring is driven by the desire to help others. Not only do you help others; you also benefit yourself.

If you grew up with ADHD you have a unique perspective on life. Many people say the difference between success and failure is a good teacher. No one has more invested in the area of ADHD than people who have been through it. No one has more personal insights and stories to offer individuals with ADHD than people who have been through it. Being a mentor—passing on your knowledge, understanding, and support—can be a powerful thing not only for an individual needing help but also for the person doing the helping.

Mentoring is the act of giving advice, teaching, or helping a usually less experienced individual who is in the process of learning something. Peer mentors are people who have been in a similar experience as someone else and are helping that less-experienced person learn the way. Mentoring programs are common. One you may have heard of is Big Brothers/Big Sisters. In many colleges and graduate programs, a more experienced student is paired with younger and less experienced students. ADHD is no different. There are also mentoring programs for ADHD. Some colleges offer peer-mentoring programs for students with ADHD. Many people who struggled in school attribute their success to a peer who cared or a teacher who helped them. As a person with ADHD you have a unique opportunity to give support and help to someone in the process of learning about ADHD and what he will need to do to thrive. In other words, your superpower is your knowledge and compassion for others as they find their way.

Mentors can make difficulties seem normal; help you adjust to new environments, integrate socially, connect to services, and reduce your sense of isolation. They can tell you about difficulties you may face in the future, and they can listen when you are having a tough time. In other words, by helping others you can become a superhero in someone else's life. That is a real superpower. You do not need to have ADHD to be a mentor to someone who has it, but can you think of a better person to do it? That is why mentoring is the last superpower, one that can make you a superhero to someone else.

But wait, that isn't it. Being a mentor to someone else not only benefits them; it can benefit you as well. Did you know that research has shown that mentors themselves have increased in school connectedness, self-esteem, empathy, and their own coping skills; they also learned more about child development. Mentoring others not only helps the people they mentor; it makes mentors better people as well.[21] Studies show that the reason most people volunteer is because of strong personal values and also to develop a better understanding of themselves and others. It makes sense that modeling being comfortable with ADHD and practicing leadership skills will benefit you as well.

An example of a college that used a peer mentoring program was Lehigh University. Peers were upper classmen with diagnosed learning disabilities. They were paired up with lower classmen who had learning disabilities and also the same major because the upper classmen had most likely taken the same courses. The peer mentoring program resulted in higher retention rates after first semester and higher GPAs.[22]

SUCCESSFUL PEOPLE WITH ADHD

There are many well-known people with ADHD. Several attribute some of their success to having ADHD. Some of the traits that were discussed in the superpowers chapter were creativity, hyperfocus, persistence, and sense of humor. These are some of the same traits that people say helped them to become successful. Having ADHD has also been challenging for many of these people. Maybe you share some of the same struggles in school and in life that they have.

It is one thing to read about ADHD, symptoms, history, and social and emotional impacts, but it is another to hear it from those who have gone through the same experiences as you. Reading about people who have overcome similar challenges as you can be helpful for a number of reasons. It can be inspiring and motivating to know that others have overcome similar challenges. Stories from others can make you feel you are not the only ones who have had these experiences, that you are not alone. Also hearing the advice of others who have been through similar experiences can allow you to learn from their mistakes and not make them. Hopefully hearing their words will make you understand that it gets better.

When you are young, school is one of the most important parts of your life. You spend most of your waking hours there. School is where you make your friends, learn, play sports, do hobbies, and more. Some have a harder time in school because of problems learning or ADHD. It should be no surprise that many of the successful people in this chapter tell stories involving school. School can be a hard place for someone with ADHD and can sometimes make you feel like you don't fit in. Even though school is hard, many people with ADHD really enjoy learning. What can be really frustrating is that their grades and test scores may not reflect what they have learned. Getting poor grades can leave some kids with ADHD feeling that they have failed. The good news is that there are others just like you who may have struggled in school. For them, success was something that they were still able to achieve.

With over eighty million books in print, Captain Underpants is one of the most successful children's book series of all time. Author and illustrator Dave Pilkey invented Captain Underpants while in grammar school; he was a student

Successful People with ADHD

- Dave Pilkey—creator author of the Captain Underpants book series
- Channing Tatum—actor
- Michael Phelps—Olympic swimmer
- Simone Biles—Olympic gymnast
- Greg LeMond—pro cycler
- Lisa Ling—journalist
- Adam Levine—musician and TV host
- David Neeleman—CEO and entrepreneur
- Scott Kelly—NASA astronaut
- Will.i.am—music writer, producer, and performer
- Dave Farrow—world memory champion
- Paul Orfelia—CEO and entrepreneur
- Ty Pennington—TV host and builder
- Glenn Beck—radio and TV commentator
- Ned Hallowell—medical doctor and author

with both ADHD and dyslexia. Dave, who refers to ADHD as attention-deficit/ hyperactivity delightfulness, was a self-admitted poorly behaved student. He was kicked out of his class for poor behavior so often that he had his own desk in the hallway.

> I had such a hard time as a kid growing up in school, feeling like an out-sider, feeling very alone, and feeling like I had so many challenges and feeling like a failure. And I know that there are a lot of kids out there that are going through some of those feelings as well. Even though there are so many more resources out there. It's very common for kids to feel alone with their challenges. I think it would have been very helpful for me to know that you can have challenges and you can still turn out OK. That was something I didn't really hear too much of when I was a kid, and I wasn't sure that things would work out for me but there are so many resources out there, if you look online . . . people who had ADHD or have dyslexia and grew up and turned out OK and became successful. I think it's impor-tant to look at the success stories and to realize that . . . there is hope for everyone. If I could go back I would have talked to myself and said, don't worry everything is going to work out okay.[1]

At a speech to a group of teachers at a Scholastic book conference, Dave described two defining moments of his school career:

> In second grade I had a lot of behavior problems. Nowadays they call it ADHD; back then they didn't have a label for it but I was definitely ADHD with an extra helping of H, so it was kind of rough being a second grader. . . . My teacher moved a desk out into the hallway for me because of my inappropriate behavior in school. And in the classroom, of course, every single day I would be like doing something goofy—like you're all teachers, you know this one [farts with his hands]; that was one of my favorites—so my teacher would say to me, "Mr. Pilkey, out" and I would go out into the hallway and I had this desk out there. The desk was like a flip top desk and I would flip it open and I would keep it filled up with pencils and papers and markers and things and it was kind of cool because I knew every day I was going to be sent out into the hallway, for a few hours, and I had a lot of time on my hands so I began to draw pictures out in the hallway and after a while I began to write stories too and I made these stories into comic books and I would bring these back into the classroom to share with my friends and the teacher didn't really like that too much and I remember one time she took one of my comics right from me and she ripped it up and she took me outside and she said to me . . . , "Mr. Pilkey you've gotta grow up because you can't spend the rest of your life making silly books" and . . . luckily I wasn't a very good listener. And that was one of the defining moments of my childhood.[2]

This was a defining moment because during this school year he created Captain Underpants.

The other defining moment was in high school; it was very similar, "I had a principal who was a horrible, just an awful person, and it was a kind of a similar situation, I was drawing in class, and he took me outside in the hall and he said, 'Dave, I know you think you're special because you can draw, but I want to tell you that artists are a dime a dozen, and you will never make a living as an artist.' . . . The thing is that every single day was kind of like that for me but those are the two days that I really remember."[3] Dave credits this principal as the inspiration for the character Mr. Krupp, who is one of the central characters in the books and is the person who turns into Captain Underpants. There is no doubt that Dave's school life was important to him for many reasons, but also it was important to Dave to tell students now that it gets better and to do what you love to do.

Actor Channing Tatum is best known for his parts in movies like *Magic Mike*, *Step Up*, and *21 Jump Street*. However, he also has ADHD and dyslexia. When talking about his experience in school he said,

I was really bad in school. . . . I got tested a bunch of times for just learning disabilities and all kinds of stuff and ultimately, I think it was just a combination of ADD and dyslexia or some version of it. . . . It gets really discouraging when you are the last one to get up from taking a test like every single time. Then I probably looked at it as I thought I was stupid or something. I thought I had some disability because they literally label it as a disability. I am actually thankful for it now; I think it has helped me. I attribute it a lot to my creativity. I think my mind does work differently; it helps me a lot with acting and thinking quickly. And focusing; it has been my fight my whole life just focusing my attention and dedicating myself to something if I want to do it.[4]

Channing describes what many say is a struggle to pay attention and focus in class, and also feeling bad about the challenges of school including difficulty with tests.

Olympic swimming champion Michael Phelps has discussed the fact that he has ADHD. © *Photofest*

Another successful person who has ADHD is Olympic champion swimmer Michael Phelps. Michael, the most decorated Olympian of all time, has competed in five Olympics and he has a record twenty-eight medals, twenty-three of them gold (also a record). However, Michael also has ADHD, which was diagnosed when he was young. He has described himself as somebody that was always bouncing off the walls and that he could never sit still. When asked what advice he would give to his younger self about his struggles in school, he had this to say:

> If I could go back in time and tell my younger self something I would tell him to believe what is in his heart and never ever give up. That is something that I have lived with my whole entire life and will continue to live with. It has been something that has changed my life since the beginning. I think the biggest thing for me, once I found that it was OK to talk to somebody and seek help. I think that is something that has changed my life forever. And now I am able to live life to its fullest.[5]

Recalling a story from his school days, Michael said, "I had kids who were in the same class and teachers would treat them differently than they would treat me. I had a teacher tell me that I 'would never amount to anything,' and I 'would never be successful.' So it was a challenge and it was a struggle, but for me it was something that I'm thankful happened and I'm thankful I am how I am and I look at myself every day and I am so proud and so happy at who I am and who I have been able to become."[6]

Michael touches on an important topic that it is OK to talk about having ADHD, and it is also OK to get help when you need it. Often there can be a stigma attached to mental health that can prevent people from talking about it and from seeking help. Listening to those who have told others and been helped can give others the courage to do so.

Simone Biles is an Olympic gymnast who has won four medals—three gold, including the all-around gold. Simone was also diagnosed with ADHD as a child. Simone discusses her diagnosis of ADHD at the age of nine. "At the time I didn't feel a lot different from other kids. I just had a short attention span so I always had to be doing something and I got distracted easily. It's never held me back through anything and I've never let it hold me back." She goes on to explain, "Don't think of anything as a downfall. Think of it as a superpower."[7] Some people prefer to look at the positive aspects of ADHD as superpowers as you read in chapter 9.

Not everyone is diagnosed as a child; some go through their entire lives before realizing that they have ADHD. Once they realize they have ADHD the diagnosis can help to explain why school or other activities have always been so hard. How well we do in school is an example of this. When we do not do well in school, we often try to find a reason why. If we do not know we have ADHD, we may look for other reasons—"Maybe I'm lazy. Maybe I'm stupid. Maybe I have a bad teacher. I think the work is boring." Sometimes finding out that there is a reason that school was so hard can be like an a-ha moment that can explain years of difficulty instantly.

Greg LeMond is an entrepreneur, inventor, and ex-professional bicycle racer who's very successful cycling career included winning the Tour de France three times. Greg did not realize that he had ADHD until later in life and describes his experience:

> ADD was getting out in the news and one of the teachers recommended for one of my kids to see a doctor for ADD and as they were getting examined, I read this thing—20 questions—and I check, check, check, check. I had every one of them. So, and now I look back and I laugh at it because it's like, of course because it explains a lot of stuff. It stood out like a sore thumb, my childhood, it was just the classic kid that couldn't pay attention, couldn't stand still in his seat, and I said that I was always, not in trouble . . . but always . . . not trouble trouble, like doing really bad things but mischief. But it always got me to the principals . . . it was very frustrating and really lowers your self-esteem. I had a sister that was really good in school so it just made me feel like an idiot.[8]

He states that now as an adult, "I realize that I am not dumb. I have capabilities of learning, I have my own set of intelligence. I wish I would have had somebody there to tell me, you're smart, you just need a different tactic, a different way of learning."[9]

Greg described cycling as an activity that helped him concentrate. He said that it "took a fog off my brain," he was "able to absorb stuff I read," and it changed his life.[10]

Greg also pointed out that having ADHD and other learning problems can have an impact on your self-esteem. Learning that he was not stupid or lazy helped him to feel better about himself. That is one of the benefits of reading these stories: you can hear it directly from someone that has experienced it. You are smart, too, and you can do well; you may just need a different style of learning.

Journalist Lisa Ling also discusses finding out as an adult that she had ADHD.

> My head is kind of spinning but I feel a little bit of relief because for so long I've been fighting it and been so frustrated with this inability to focus. . . . It's been such a source of frustration for me. . . . As a journalist when I am immersed in a story, then I feel like I can laser focus but if I'm not working my mind goes in every direction but where it is supposed to go.

I've been like that since I was a kid. [In elementary school] my teacher was calling my dad to meetings all of the time to say I had focus issues. [In high school] I could go through an entire period and not retain a sentence if I weren't interested in the topic or the subject matter.[11]

Adam Levine, the lead singer of Maroon 5 and judge on the television show *The Voice*, was diagnosed as a teen and went to get reevaluated as an adult to find that he had adult ADHD. "I struggled with ADHD throughout my life. It was hard for me to sit down, focus, and get schoolwork done. . . . My struggles continued as an adult. I had trouble sometimes writing songs and recording in the studio. I couldn't always focus and complete everything I had to. . . . So I went back to the doctor to discuss my symptoms, and I learned that I still had ADHD. It was affecting my career the way it had affected me in school. . . . ADHD doesn't go away when you grow older."[12]

David Neeleman was the president of Southwest Airlines and also the CEO and founder of JetBlue Airlines. His innovations include having TV screens on the back of every airline seat, leather seats for coach, and also the electronic ticket, or e-ticket. David was not formally diagnosed with ADHD until he was an adult and chose not to take any medication. He describes the fact that he can hire people to organize his daily routines and that he had already learned to cope with his symptoms by the time he received his diagnosis:

ADHD is a two-edged sword and I didn't even really know I had it until I was in my midthirties. I felt like, "Geez, why can't I just calm down and just be content?" You know with what I have, and so my mom, my brother, my younger brother had been diagnosed with ADD, and so my mom sent me this book and said why don't you read it? And I can't possibly get through the whole book but the book was called *Driven to Distraction*. It was written by Dr. Hallowell, and so I just turned to a page that had the twenty-one characteristics of somebody who had ADHD and I had twenty of the twenty-one, and I was just like . . . , "Oh that's it, that's what it is." So I learned more about it . . . and got officially diagnosed. . . . It can drive you completely insane if you don't control it. . . . On the negative side you're flying all over the place you can't get anything done; you can't even pay your bills and all that kind of stuff. But on the other side, you just have this hyperfocus.[13]

Dave said that people ask him, what to do with their own children who have ADHD, and he said, "You know what I do with my son with ADHD, and how do I help him succeed? I say, have him find a passion, something that he is totally passionate about and he'll be better than anyone else at it. . . . Let him do something

Will Smith described himself in school as "the fun one who had trouble paying attention. Today they'd diagnose me as a child with ADHD. I was a B student who should've been getting As. Classic underachiever. It was hard for me to read an entire book in two weeks. Today I buy a book and have someone read it for me on tape!" Source: Nancy Collins, "Will Smith: Big Willie Style," *Rolling Stone Magazine*, 1998. *NBC / Photofest © NBC*

that he loves. And they will be better at it than anyone else, they will focus on it so much no one will be able to compete with him.[14]

David makes reference to hyperfocus that was discussed in chapter 1. Hyperfocus is the ability to have long uninterrupted times of focus on areas of interest. It is a trait that many people with ADHD refer to, and one that Dave thinks is important to success.

Scott Kelly is an American astronaut who spent 520 days in space. He has been involved in research to find out what the long-term effects of space are on the human body. This is an area of research that will eventually help humans as they travel in space for longer and longer periods of time. Scott Kelly also acknowledges that if he were in school now he would have been diagnosed with ADHD. Scott's story stresses that he did not let his poor performance early in school stop him from doing what he wanted. He did not let his challenges in school limit his choices in what he wanted to do for a living. He literally reached for the stars. As David Neeleman stated, he picked a profession that he was very passionate about and nothing could stop him, even poor grades and challenges in school.

When talking about how other astronauts probably got good grades, Scott said,

I was the exact opposite, did very poorly in school, couldn't pay attention. You know if I was in school today I'd be the kid with ADD, ADHD. [I] sat in the back of the class looking out the window. Went to college and did bad there and then one day I was walking into the bookstore to buy gum or something, not a book but I saw this book on the shelf. . . . It had a red white and blue cover, had a really cool title, made me pick it up. I looked at the back, started paging through it and it was *The Right Stuff* by Tom Wolfe, and I thought, "You know I feel like I have a lot in common with these guys with one big exception: I can't do my homework, and if I can fix that one problem, maybe I can be like them and fly in space one day."[15]

Scott and David are not the only people with ADHD who credit passion for their jobs as a major motivator, source of happiness, and way to cope with ADHD. Will.i.am is a member of the music group Black Eyed Peas. He is a music writer and producer, has won seven Grammy awards, and has sold millions of albums and downloads. He describes his coping with ADHD through his music:

A lot of kids have that ADD or whatever you want to call it—attention disorder. I just figured out a way to keep my attention disorder in order. I can be thinking about the song, thinking about the guy who just raised his hand up there looking at that little light that's blinking, and I'm thinking about, "Do I really want to drink the orange juice? Oh gosh, I have to DJ at 12:30 tonight. What am I gonna play? Is apple gonna be there?" All this stuff is in my head at the same time as I'm doin it. I don't know how to stop, I don't know how to slow down, so it's not escape; it's just order. I make an order out of a disorder, and I'm not taking Ritalin; I'm taking music and the side effect is tinnitus I got beeeeeeeeeeeeeeeep every day, all day every day.[16]

Another person with ADHD, Dave Farrow, is a two-time Guinness World Record holder for memory. He has successfully memorized a random sequence of fifty-nine separate decks of playing cards consecutively. Dave talks about his experiences growing up and in school:

I was diagnosed with ADHD and dyslexia. I really struggled in focusing, and it wasn't for lack of trying. I put in so much effort but there really was a biological thing that I was trying to overcome and any of you who know about the educational system, especially if you know the way it was 10 or 20 years ago—I feel like we have made some positive changes, but in those days there was a real tendency to classify kids more than really try to transform them or change them and I'm glad to see that that's really starting to change. But I was just labeled and . . . this is still even hard for me to talk about today because I've got a boy of my own and I wonder what he is going to go through because ADHD is pretty genetic.

I had a situation with a teacher when I was fourteen, fifteen years old and he essentially wanted to set me straight. He wanted to say you know what, lower your expectations. Should anyone ever say that to a thirteen-year-old fourteen-year-old kid? Lower your expectations; don't expect much out of life because you have these learning challenges so you know just try to do the bare minimum. What a motivational speech. But you know what the odd thing is that guy actually motivated me more than anybody I've ever witnessed in my whole life. What made this worse was that I went to a parent-teacher talk—if you can remember being a kid you go with your parents to these parent teacher things—and he was talking to my mom and he was saying the same things, and I still remember to this day. I could bring back the words almost word for word: "You know, don't expect much out of your son. Try to be patient. We are going to put him in different programs"; that sort of thing and my mom actually was very polite and kind, and when he left, she turned to me and said, "You don't listen to a word that bugger ever says"—and she didn't use the word bugger, so that really motivated me. So that really motivated me. Oh my god, I mean, . . . from then on I became obsessed with improving my own memory and focus. . . . And I did pretty well at that and I actually developed a new way to study and it led me into the Guinness Book of Records. I memorized the exact order of fifty-nine decks of playing cards—all of those cards (that's 3,016 cards in total) after seeing them only once.[17]

Another entrepreneur and businessman, Paul Orfelia, started the company Kinko's. The name of the company was a reference to his red kinky hair. It was sold to FedEx in 2004 for 2.4 billion dollars.[18] Paul talks about having dyslexia and also being restless as a child.

I am extremely restless. I don't know how to sit still. Always in trouble; I could not sit still. I was expelled from John Burroughs Junior High School, anybody know where that is? Mr. McNamara told my mother, "You know, Mrs. Orfelia, one day if Paul really applies himself, he can learn to lay carpet." And so, my mom thought I could do a little more in life than that, but that was going to be my highest aspiration. Graduated from high school eighth from the bottom of my class out of 1,200 from Birmingham High School, I don't know how eight people beat me out for number one.[19]

Then Paul talks about having the choice of going to college or going into the military and he chose college. He got a chance to go to community college, which he described as a place for second chances and where he liked a course in accounting. He then attended a satellite campus of USC. "Just barely" graduating from USC, he described his learning experience as "I never took notes, I always went for a C or a D, but I could honestly say I learned in school, if I bothered learning it, I remembered it. And I enjoyed my education. I cut school, I really enjoyed learning, but I found like Mark Twain said, sometimes school really interferes with your education."[20]

Ty Pennington, who was the host of popular television show *Extreme Makeover: Home Edition*, also describes his trouble with school when he was young: "When I was in elementary school my mother received countless phone calls from my teachers, my principal's office, and even my guidance counselors because I was constantly in trouble for something. Whether it was running around the classroom, jumping from the window sill, or just not finishing my classwork, it seemed as though I could never really consistently work to my potential. My teachers pretty much insisted I was bright but I just couldn't sit still. I couldn't control my impulsive behaviors or concentrate long enough to complete tasks or even listen to simple instructions."[21]

Ty explains how he was evaluated and given the diagnosis of ADHD. However, at first, he did not know about his diagnosis and was not treated for it. He says,

[I learned to] cope with my symptoms by channeling my energy into my passion, which is building things, the bigger the better. While these creative outlets helped me control my hyperactive and impulsive behaviors I still had trouble focusing and finishing things that I really wasn't interested in. Getting through high school was a struggle academically as well as socially. It wasn't until after I dropped out of my first year of college that my mother realized how much ADHD was impacting me and how it got to other people in my life to have a negative opinion of me. So she sat me down and told me I had ADHD and suggested that I talk to my doctor. Well hearing I had ADHD really kind of hit home and everything started to make sense to me. My impulsive behaviors, my relationship or lack thereof, and my lack of focus and organization.[22]

Ty later describes that he went to his doctor and explored taking medication to treat his ADHD.

Radio and television personality Glenn Beck also describes himself as having ADHD. During a conversation with Ty Pennington, he said, "I'm riddled with ADD. I believe a lot of my ADD has led to my success. But to be able to regulate it in such a way to where you don't drive everybody out of their mind crazy around you. . . . I believe that my success in business is because I can process a million things at a time and move very rapidly but my failure at home is because of ADD."[23]

When asked if he was torn by ADD or if he saw it as only a bad thing, referring to his home life, Glenn said, "The first time that I took any kind of ADD medicine . . . I wept because I played with my son on the floor for forty minutes and I had never done that with any of my children. It was, it was night and day."[24]

Many people like Glenn choose to take medication and find it effective. Others choose not to take medication, and some choose to take it sometimes and not others. When asked about taking medication when he was younger, actor Vince Vaughn shared a different opinion:

When I was in school I was not a very good student and I had a lot of learning disabilities. I was recommended to be put on prescription drugs but I was very lucky that my dad said no and didn't want me to go through life doped up.

I had to go to a special class once a day, which was really embarrassing when you're younger. To have your name called over the loudspeaker to the office. Because the kids look at you differently and that makes you feel bad about yourself.

As I got older I was invited to this school in Washington, DC, that teaches kids with learning disabilities. The funny thing is there are really successful people who had learning disabilities, like CEOs of medical companies.[25]

Do these stories surprise you? Many of the successful people in this chapter have had some negative experiences in school. You may be left asking yourself, how did their teachers miss the fact that they were so talented or would achieve such great things? As many of these individuals learned, lack of early success in school was not an indicator of the success that they would have later in life. It is clear from their stories that some of the negative experiences that they had early in school stuck with them forever. The successful people in this chapter still remember some of the negative comments they heard from their teachers, even though they have achieved great success. Hopefully their stories can inspire you to follow your own passions in life.

BULLYING

....

Bullying is a topic that we hear about all the time. We hear about it on TV, online, in social media, and in school. You may ask yourself, what does this topic have to do with ADHD? Unfortunately some people bully individuals who are thought of as different. Some consider young people with ADHD to be different, which can make them a target. Young people with ADHD are more likely to be bullied than other students. Being victimized is only part of the problem. You may also witness someone else being victimized or you may be the bully yourself! That makes bullying a topic for everyone. In this chapter we will answer several questions about bullying: What is it? Why does it happen? What can you do about it?

What Is Bullying?

Bullying has a very specific definition. There may be times we see people being unkind to one another, by name calling, or making fun of others. These can be examples of bullying but not always. There are three parts to the definition of bullying:

1. It is aggressive and unwanted behavior intended to harm, intimidate, or humiliate.
2. It is repetitive and causes severe emotional trauma.
3. There is an imbalance of power between the person bullying and the person being bullied.[1]

Bullying is more that someone not being nice to you. The behavior has to be unwanted and repetitive, and there must be an imbalance of power. This means that a single unpleasant interaction with someone is not bullying. Even a fight between two people may not be bullying because there has to be an imbalance of power.

What this means is bullies may be bigger, stronger, older, have more social connections, hold positions of authority, or be better in school or sports. This does not mean she is better at everything, but rather an imbalance exists in some way. Many times when grown-ups think of bullying they think of the kid on the schoolyard who is taking lunches, cutting in line, and beating kids up when the teacher is not looking. Although this is also bullying, the definition of bullying has evolved over the years.

Types of Bullying

There are four main types of bullying:

1. Physical: when someone or a group of people grabs, hits, bumps, spits, pushes, takes someone's stuff, or engages in any other physical act that is not wanted
2. Social: when someone or a group of people is mean to another person, excludes him or her, makes fun, or engages in any other unwanted social activity
3. Verbal: when someone or a group of people taunts, says mean things, yells, or makes fun
4. Cyber: when someone or a group of people engages in flaming, false friend making, posting pictures, sending negative texts, outing, or sending negative emails

Aggressive Behavior

There are additional terms that involve aggressive behavior but may not meet the definition of bullying. Although a bully can be aggressive or violent, he or she is more than this. This does not mean that aggression is less serious or has less of a physical, social, or emotional impact on us. Aggressive behaviors may be a part of bullying.[2]

Peer conflict: The word conflict describes a disagreement or fight between two peers. Without a power imbalance or repetition this would not be considered bullying.[3]

Hazing: Hazing involves the use of embarrassing or dangerous activities to initiate someone into a group.[4] Hazing is a form of bullying, but it differs in certain ways. Bullying is generally meant to exclude someone from a group, while hazing is generally meant as a right of passage to join a group. Hazing is generally a pressured activity where there is an expectation by a group to perform or the person will be excluded or lose some status in the group. Many examples of hazing happen in high school or in college where some students may be over the age of eighteen and some under. Since hazing is coerced and many do not understand the consequences of saying no, it is not considered to be voluntary.[5]

Harassment: Bullying and harassment sometimes overlap, but not all bullying is harassment and not all harassment is bullying. Harassment is a legal term that means unwelcome conduct based on race, national origin, color, sex, age, disability, or religion that is severe, pervasive, or persistent and creates a hostile environment.[6] Harassment shares some characteristics with bullying. As we will learn later some people harass others for the same reason that they bully. In some states, antibullying legislation includes harassment in the definition of bullying, for example, the New Jersey HIB (harassment, intimidation, bullying) legislation.

Stalking: Stalking is repeated harassing or threatening behavior, such as following a person, damaging a person's property, or making harassing phone calls.[7]

Cyberbullying

Cyberbullying is a relatively new form of bullying compared to the other forms. It is different because it does not take place face-to-face but rather through the use of digital communication, web postings, texts, or tweets. Cyberbullying is primarily a means of engaging in social or verbal bullying.[8]

A person who cyberbullies can harass, intimidate, spread rumors, impersonate, trick, "out," or exclude. People use text messaging, email, social network sites, and other forms of electronic communication to cyberbully.[9] Cyberbullying has some unique aspects that make it more difficult to prevent and can lead to the bullying possibly lasting longer.

- Cyberbullying can be anonymous. The person does not ever have to reveal who he is or may lie about who he is. This can cause added anxiety to the person who is bullied.
- Cyberbullying is not face-to-face. The person who bullies will not see the reaction or response of the person. The person who bullies may not know what effect the bullying has on the person being bullied. This can lead the cyberbully to do or say things that she would not do or say in person.
- Cyberbullying may be accessible and viewable online for long periods of time, anytime. Information that is disclosed on the Internet can be permanent and unable to be erased; it can be repeated forever.
- Bullying online can occur 24/7, 365 days a year. In the past bullies only had access to the people they bullied during or directly after school. Cyberbullying can occur anytime, even while you are at home.

Social media can be a great way to connect with others who are going through similar experiences as you. © *iStock / seb_ra*

- The audience for the bully is limitless: messages, pictures, or another bullying method can be viewed by an infinite number of people anywhere in the world, giving the bully a potentially large stage.

For these reasons, cyberbullying is a unique form of bullying. There are also some unique terms that apply to it:

Flaming is a technique that is used online to start fights or evoke strong emotions from individuals. A flamer will write mean or provocative statements to people on social media or in comment sections. Sometimes a flamer will write negative things about a topic that others may like. Sometimes flamers will use profanity or information they know about someone to attack them.[10]

Trickery involves gaining someone's trust so you can share his or her secrets online.

Outing involves sharing secrets or embarrassing information online.

Cyberstalking is repeated or intense harassment online.

Sexting means sending sexually explicit messages or photos by phone or Internet.

Trolling involves making a deliberately offensive or provocative online post with the aim of upsetting someone or eliciting an angry response from them.

Exclusion means leaving someone out from an online group.

Sally's Story

Sally is a thirteen-year-old who tried out for and made the softball team. A group of girls has been on the team for two years, including the captain. They think Sally is not good enough to be on the team. They have been excluding her from after-school activities, sending her nasty emails, and flaming her online. The other girls want her to quit the team and will continue to do this until she quits. What do you think?

This seems to be a case of bullying, both social and cyber. Although Sally is new on the team, this is not hazing because the girls do not want her to be on the team and their behavior is not a tradition or right of passage. The girls are socially excluding Sally and also sending her emails and flaming her on social media. The actions of the group are definitely unwanted and repeated, and there is also an imbalance of power. There are more of the other girls than Sally and they are well established on the team, whereas Sally is a newcomer.

Who Is Involved in Bullying?

Bullying is more than just the bully and the person who is bullied. There are other people involved too. Sometimes those other people can add to the problem, help stop it, or just watch. As you read about who is involved in bullying, think about times in your life when you might have been any of these people.

Bullying is a behavior, and behaviors can be learned, unlearned, and changed. When we describe a person, we should use the language "a person who bullies" or "a person who was bullied" rather than call them "a bully" or "a victim." Using person-first language puts the emphasis on the fact that people are people and not the sum of their actions, abilities, or disabilities. However, people who bully and people who are bullied are not the only people involved. It is everyone's job to create an open and accepting environment to prevent bullying from happening. Here are some definitions of others who are involved in bullying.

Bystander—someone who witnesses bullying

Upstander—someone who witnesses bullying and speaks up or against the bullying

Frallies—a combination of the words *friend* and *ally*; a person who stands with you against bullying

Kids who assist—people who are not leading the bullying but still watch, encourage, and occasionally join in

Kids who reinforce—children who do not lead the bullying but provide an audience by laughing, watching, or encouraging it to continue[11]

Statistics on Bullying

Gathering bullying information can be difficult because sometimes people do not like to report that they have been bullied or that they bully. For that reason statistics on bullying have been inconsistent. According to the National Center for Educational Statistics (NCES) about 20 percent of students grades 6 through 12 claimed that they had been bullied.

Of the students that had been bullied, almost all reported that they had experienced verbal or social bullying and about 13 percent said that they had been made fun of, called names, or insulted. In addition, 12 percent of students reported that they had rumors spread about them, about 5 percent reported that they had been physically bullied (pushed, shoved, tripped, or spit on), and 1.8 percent reported that their property was destroyed on purpose. Finally, 5 percent of students reported that they were excluded from activities on purpose, 4 percent reported that they were threatened with harm, and 2.5 percent said someone tried to make them do things they did not want to do.[12]

Where Students Are Bullied

Bullying can occur in many different places, but according to the NCES, the majority of it occurred in school: 41 percent of students reported being bullied in a hallway or stairwell, 33 percent of students reported being bullied in a classroom, 22 percent in the cafeteria, and 19 percent outside on school grounds. Finally, 11.5 percent of students reported being bullied online or in text, 10 percent on the school bus, and 9 percent of students reported being bullied in a locker room. Cyberbullying was reported more often in older students than in younger.[13]

How Often Are Students Bullied?

Of the students that reported being bullied, 66 percent reported it happened once or twice in the school year, 19 percent reported that they were bullied once or twice a month, 10 percent reported once or twice a week, and 4 percent reported almost every day. When it came to adults being notified, 43 percent of students reported that an adult was notified in the case of bullying. However, there was a big difference in the rate of reporting, for example, 60 percent of bullying was reported to an adult in sixth grade but only 26 percent of bullying was reported in the twelfth grade.[14]

Negative Effects of Bullying

Being exposed to bullying can have negative effects on you—living in constant anticipation, watching others get bullied, or being afraid that you will be next are all negative experiences. Being in this type of environment for extended periods can leave someone feeling anxious or afraid. Being in an environment where there is a culture of bullying can also distort the way you think about yourself. If you fear that you will be victimized because of your likes or hobbies, enjoyable activities may seem less enjoyable and you might avoid them altogether.

Since bullying frequently happens at school, one of the consequences can be a negative impact on schoolwork, which can mean lower grades. Of students who reported being bullied, 13 percent reported a negative effect on schoolwork, 14 percent reported a negative effect on relationships with family and friends, 20 percent reported negative feelings about self, and 9 percent reported a decline in physical health. Being bullied has been linked to increased rates of depression.[15] In high school people exposed to bullying are more likely to miss school and have increased absences. Some children who are bullied are less likely to attend college. Being bullied affects how we deal with stress and may leave us open to mental health problems in the future.[16] Constant worrying, fear, or witnessing others being bullied can create a stressful environment that is not healthy for anyone.

Perceived Cause of Bullying

There is no single reason that some people get bullied or why some choose to do it. When reporting why they thought it had happened, 27 percent of students who were bullied said it was because of their appearance, 10 percent because of race, 4 percent because of religion, 7 percent because of ethnic origin, 7 percent because of gender, 4 percent because of disability, and 3 percent because of sexual orientation. Many times people are bullied because of perceived differences between themselves and everyone else.[17] Sometimes behavior that is linked to ADHD can look like a difference and be a factor in students with ADHD being bullied.

Who Is Getting Bullied?

In surveys, about 30 percent of students admit that they have bullied others, and about 70 percent of students say that they have witnessed it. When bystanders intervene, bullying stops more than half of the time within a few seconds. However, there are definite risk factors for being bullied.[18]

Children who are bullied may be perceived as different from others. This could be due to the way they look, their weight, their clothing, being new in school, or having less money than other students. Students who are perceived as weak or unable to defend themselves may also be targets of bullying. Students who appear to be anxious, depressed, or have low self-esteem may be targets of bullies. Students who are less popular or have few friends are targets. Finally, students who do not get along with others, are considered annoying, or antagonize others may be the victims of bullying.[19] Some of these behaviors or differences have been associated with ADHD and can make students with ADHD targets of bullying more often.

Why Bully?

You may ask yourself, why would someone choose to bully? Does it make them feel good or better about themselves? Not everyone is the same or does it for the same reason. Some studies have identified that bullies generally fall into one of two categories: popular and "lone wolf." Although this is an oversimplification, since people who bully can fall anywhere between these two descriptions, it offers us a way to understand different reasons people do it.

Popular bullies are socially well connected, have friends, and like to be in charge of others. These people are concerned with their popularity. This last point is important because in order for you to be popular and be liked, you cannot be *all bad*. These types of bullies typically mix prosocial behaviors (being nice, doing favors, sticking up for people, offering apologies) with antisocial behaviors (being mean, excluding). Within social groups they may bully enough to gain dominance, but not too much or no one will like them. They may single out peers and gang up on them.[20] Lone wolf bullies are less popular; they may have depression, anxiety, or low self-esteem and may not have empathy toward others.

Certain characteristics have been identified that many bullies share: they are aggressive or easily frustrated, have less parental involvement or have problems at home, think badly of others, have difficulty following rules, view violence in a positive way, and have friends who bully others.[21] Students with ADHD have higher rates of being bullied and also bullying. This means that in addition to being victimized, they can also fall into either of the categories above.

Why bully? Bullying can get you what you want. Some very popular kids may do it to maintain social status; some marginally popular kids may do it to raise their social status. The bully may mix more prosocial behaviors with antisocial ones and get others to rally around him when he singles individuals out. The goal may be to maintain cohesion for their social clique. Some bullies may ignore social rules or impulsively act aggressively to get things that they want, which may work and reinforce the aggressive behavior. Some may do it so that they are not bullied themselves.

The environment also has something to do with how people act. Just like any behavior, bullying comes with risks and consequences. In some environments the risk is low and there are almost no consequences for bullying. Environments with no adult supervision, no rules, or anyone to enforce the rules are very low-risk for bullying behavior. In other words, there may not be any consequences for doing it. In addition, in some environments bullying may make someone look popular and powerful. This would make bullying seem socially rewarding and more likely to happen.

There are many reasons why people bully, so the answer to this question is not easy or simple. Bullying can get something the student wants or increase social standing, or maybe the culture of the school or environment promotes or rewards bullying. Whatever the reason that a student or a group of students chooses to bully, there are environmental factors that can make it easier to do.

Bullying and ADHD

What does all of this bullying have to do specifically with ADHD? Good question. It has been reported that children with ADHD have four times the chance of being bullies and ten times the chance of being bullied.[22] This number is higher than the average number of students without ADHD who report they have been bullied at some point. If you have ADHD, this is an important difference to be aware of.

Research on bullying has also found that among the three groups—bullied, bystander, and bully—the two groups most likely to switch places are the bully and the bullied. This means that in some cases individuals who have been bullied have also been bullies. This is not an excuse for the bullying behavior, which is never OK; however, it does help to understand that frequently a bully may have at one time been a victim of bullying.

In all of the antibullying laws passed in the United States, it is recommended that there be provisions for the delivery of mental health services for anyone who has been involved in bullying when it is reported, including both the students being bullied and the students who bullied.[23]

Remember: bullies and the bullied have some things in common and both may have social or emotional difficulties. Luckily these types of problems can be helped with counseling and parent training. It is also important to promote an environment in school that does not reward bullying behavior with friends, social status, and higher self-esteem but rather rewards prosocial behaviors instead.

Barbara: From Being Bullied to Becoming a Bully

Barbara was a student in a public school. When she was younger she had problems with her academics. Since she was in a regular school, kids made fun of her and teased her because she could not read. As she got older it became clear that she was unable to read things that most of the other kids in her class could read. Barbara was talented at other things besides academics, including sports, and she was very social. The teasing turned into constant taunting and harassment by some students who said, "What are you, stupid? Can you even read your name?"

Barbara was evaluated, and it was discovered that she had ADHD and a learning disability. The next year she was enrolled in a special school where she could receive help for her reading. Barbara found that some students in her new school had physical disabilities, were smaller than her, and were not good at sports. Being good at sports and very social, she was able to make friends in the school; however she started making fun of other students and harassing them because of their disabilities. Barbara had switched places: she went from being bullied to being the bully.

Remember: in order for someone to do a behavior, she must have learned it somewhere and it must also work. Barbara is an example of someone who had been exposed to bullying. You may ask, "Why would someone who has been bullied bully someone else?" There are many answers to this question. The behavior works on some level, and it gets her what she wants—social status, more friends, power—or maybe it prevents others from bullying her. Whatever the reason, we must be aware that in many cases bullies have been bullied.

Antibullying and the Law

Did you know that all fifty states in the United States have antibullying legislation? It's true; although there is no federal law against bullying, every state has passed a law protecting students in school from bullying. Legislation is different in every state, although many laws contain common elements. According to Stop-Bullying.gov, bullying legislation should contain elements such as the following:

- Definitions of bullying
- Reasons individuals can be bullied
- Procedures to report bullying
- Procedures to investigate bullying
- Procedures to respond to bullying
- Procedures for documenting bullying
- Consequences for bullying
- Referral for mental health services for people who have been involved in bullying
- Communication plan to inform students and families about policies and consequences of bullying
- School trainings on bullying
- Publicly available data on bullying[24]

This means that you can know what steps you can take in your school if you have been bullied or witness bullying. Schools may differ in reporting procedures; however, verbal or written reports are usually made to designated school personnel or administrators. The reports should be investigated and remediated.

Why Don't People Report Bullying?

Bullying reporting declines with age. Students are more likely to report a bully if they think that the teachers will do something about it. So having good relationships with teachers is important. Did you know that students are less likely to report bullying if they think the bully will be punished? Kids don't report because they fear retaliation.[25]

Bullying is also not always easy to detect. Bullies can use sarcasm, double meanings, facial expressions, or subtly exclude other students from activities. Blake E. S. Taylor, a student with ADHD, wrote in his book *ADHD and Me*, "Undercover verbal harassment is the weapon of choice among middle school students. And unlike a physical fight, where there is ample evidence, like cuts and bruises, spoken words simply vanish into the air without a trace."[26]

Blake added that when he was being bullied, he did not want to report the bully for fear of being called a tattletale, which would be humiliating. He was afraid of his reputation being ruined and then the bully making fun of him for that as well.

Questions and Answers

If I Am Being Bullied Does That Make Me Weak or a Loser?

Absolutely not. Being bullied is not your fault. Remember the person or persons doing the bullying are the ones who are wrong, not you. Knowing that you are not to blame and that no one deserves for any reason to be bullied will make it easier to do something about it.

Don't Boys Get Bullied More Often Than Girls?

False. The rates of bullying of boys to girls are very similar.

Did You Know That Individuals with a Best Friend Are Less Likely to Be Bullied?

It's true. Having a best friend is called a *protective factor* against bullying. Having a best friend is not the only protective factor; there are others. Another protective factor is having the support of your family. People with family support have lower rates of bullying.[27] Another protective factor is having a good relationship with your teachers. Having a good relationship with teachers can make it easier to report when bullying happens.

If Someone Bullies Me Shouldn't I Just Beat Them Up so They Will Stop?

Remember in order for it to be bullying there has to be an imbalance of power. Many times this imbalance makes it difficult for someone to fight back. In addition using violence against someone without reporting their bullying will most likely get you in trouble and not the bully.

Did You Know That Bullying Is More Likely to Happen in a School Where Teachers Have Poor Relationships with Students?

In schools where students and teachers talk frequently it is a protective factor against bullying.

COLLEGE AND CAREER

According to research, people with ADHD have higher rates of college drop-out than other students.[1] In addition students with ADHD use 25 percent of all the college accommodations that are given to students with disabilities. College is a big transition and there are a lot of things that you need to think about when you go there. Should you live close to home or travel? Live on campus or off campus? Should you go somewhere where you will know people or somewhere where you don't know anyone? What should you study when you get to college? Should you play sports and join groups? Who should you hang out with? These are all good questions, and you should think about them before you go to school. The answer to any of them could be yes or it could be no; however, knowing the answers to these questions can help you succeed.

College is a fresh and new experience for young adults, it is a place where you can make new friends, learn to live independently, feed your mind with knowledge and decide what you would like to be when you grow up. You will begin to

"For years I was fidgety in class, often unfocused, but I got the work done and I had good grades throughout school so nobody ever said anything. I finally asked for help when I was getting in trouble for doing or saying things that I knew were wrong. They just came out of my mouth before they went through my head. It was always something inappropriately timed or said in the wrong way. One of my teachers worked closely with my guidance counselor and me to figure out the problem and, eventually, we came to the possibility of ADHD. Since my diagnosis I have been much more focused in school and at home, getting in much less trouble, and overall I'm very happy that I was diagnosed before I finished high school, because trying to figure out college this year without knowing why I struggle with certain things would be less than successful for sure."—anonymous student[a] have many of the responsibilities of an adult. College can be a place of extreme personal growth.

These benefits do not come without challenges. College can be a very big adjustment for young adults. You may not have access to the same friends you had in high school. Maybe your family was a source of support for you and they are now far away. There is less structure requiring more organizational skills, schoolwork is harder, and there is less academic support. Peers are engaging in more risk-taking behaviors with less supervision from adults. Managing sleeping, eating, personal hygiene, healthy habits, time, money, and other self-management skills can be challenging for anyone, especially when it is the first time that you have to do it on your own.

Having ADHD is one more factor that you have to plan for when going to school. These challenges are the same for everyone, not just for young adults with ADHD. Here are some more things you may need to know.

Self-Management

All of these changes may make college a difficult transition. It can go very well or not very well. Before students go to college their families usually play a large role in their lives. When you get to college there is no one to check on you, make sure you did your homework, make sure you go to sleep on time, cook for you, or do many of the other activities that your parents may have helped with before college. Self-management skills include those that allow you to manage your own life, for example:

- Making sure you get enough sleep
- Eating healthy
- Managing money
- Getting exercise
- Scheduling
- Keeping your living space and belongings organized
- Doing laundry

It is not unusual for your family to help you with these things before college. However, when you go away, many of these responsibilities will become your own. With lots of experiences to be experienced on a daily basis, everything in college is new. This means that it is really easy for your schedule to become unpredictable, because there is always something different to do. This can make it really hard to have a reasonable bed time, healthy eating habits, and good money

College may be the first time that you will have to live on your own. Keeping your living space clean and organized is important. A functioning desk and study area will do you more good than a dirty pile of clothes. © iStock / denozy

management. Also, no one is around to make you do laundry, keep your living space organized, or remind you to do other household chores. Scheduling these tasks can be helpful because you may find something more fun to do instead, like going to a basketball game or a movie.

Many of these tasks are related to one another. For example, if you cannot manage your money and it runs out, then how will you do your laundry at the end of the week? If you do not schedule your day, how can you make sure that you will be getting enough sleep? If you do not get enough sleep you will be tired and it will be more difficult to eat healthy and exercise.

Luckily there are many ways that you can *help yourself* before you get into trouble in these areas. Most colleges have meal plans that will ensure that you have access to healthy foods, in addition in many places you can prepay for your laundry. You parents can help you with financial planning by giving you a prepaid credit card. This can help you set limits on how much you spend ahead of time. Using a weekly planner or calendar app can help you schedule times that you are supposed to be doing other tasks or sleeping. Finally having a group of friends or roommates that are like-minded helps a lot. You can schedule laundry time together, go to eat with one another, go to the gym and split the cost of activities and purchases.

Academics

Young adults with ADHD have more trouble academically in college. It has been reported that students with ADHD have lower grade point averages, increased risk of academic probation, increased withdrawal rates from classes, and increased school dropout rates. Students with ADHD have trouble taking notes, planning and completing assignments, and planning and completing long-term assignments.[2]

By knowing this before college you can make sure that you have access to accommodations from the office of student disability services. In addition, in many schools you can access student tutoring, become a part of student study groups and make sure you have regular contact with professors to help set up a realistic study schedule. Knowing the difficulties before they happen is an important part of doing well in school.

If you are eligible for accommodations in college, then talking to the campus department for students with disabilities is what you should do. If the campus offers free tutoring than get it. Peer mentoring? Sign up. If there are online support groups, join them. Get involved with campus activities and organizations that are related to your major.

"When I transferred to Cal State LA in 2008 one of the first stops I made was to the office of students with disabilities. I met with my counselor Dr. Silberstein there and I was a very nervous and awkward transfer student who was newly diagnosed with ADHD and I had no idea what that was going to mean for me and my family and my life or my education, for all I knew back then ADHD was this debilitative disease, that was going to eat away at my brain and turn me into some, like, zombie, one of the perks of ADHD is having a very vivid imagination but anyway Dr. Silberstein sits me down in his office and said something to me that I'll never forget, with a smile on his face he said, 'Angela, ADHD is not a prison sentence, you have a learning disability but you are not disabled, some people would say that you think outside the box, but its more like you don't even really know where the box is.' And I laughed, and I exhaled, and I took that mantra with me for the rest of my life."—Angela, a college student with ADHD[b]

What Should I Study in College?

You may be wondering, "What should I study in college?" (By the way, everyone wonders about the answer to this question!) And does it matter that I have ADHD? The answer is, it is up to you. There are many majors to choose from. According to the College Board, there are eight categories of college majors:

1. Arts and humanities
2. Business
3. Health and medicine
4. Multi/interdisciplinary studies
5. Public and social service
6. Science, math, and technology
7. Social sciences
8. Trades and personal services[3]

Within these large categories there are also lots and lots of different kinds of majors which can prepare you for many different types of careers. Some majors are highly specialized and prepare you for a specific type of career or graduate degree; some give you many choices when you graduate. When picking a major it is really important for you to like the field of study that you are in, because liking what you study has a positive impact on your motivation and excitement about the subject matter, which makes it easier and more enjoyable to study and learn.

Another question that you need to consider is, what are the requirements of the major? If you look at the course work and it involves a lot of studying, are you willing to do it? Maybe grading is based on more practical experience. Maybe the format of many of the classes is lecture and note-taking. Maybe a major involves a lot of lab work or field work. Is this something that you like to do? Maybe a major requires you to do a lot of public speaking. Maybe you are graded on writing. Perhaps a major requires you to be graded more on presentations than tests or on lab assignments rather than projects. These are all practical things to consider when picking a college major and also a course of study. If you plan on getting a graduate degree after college, are there GPA requirements for the programs that you would like to apply for? Are you meeting those requirements?

When picking a college major, it shouldn't matter that you have ADHD but you should be aware of what that major will require of you, and you must ask yourself, "Am I willing to put the time into this major?" or "Does it play to my gifts and abilities?"

"When I was picking a college major I had the idea that I wanted to work in the field of business and accounting. I flipped through the book with all the majors and the courses in that major looked pretty interesting to me. I went to all of the classes and found some of the course work interesting; however, almost all of the classes were lecture and note-taking, which I was not very good at. As the courses got harder I found the subject matter to be dry and boring and had a hard time paying attention to the lectures. This made note-taking really hard. The grading was almost exclusively based on tests which required me to memorize lots of stuff that I thought was useless. This made spending hours and hours of studying this material pretty much impossible.

Luckily, I had chosen a minor field of study to be communications and found that I was getting A's in almost all of the classes with way less studying and I found the subject matter way more interesting and useful, at least the books were written in English. The fact that I found the lectures interesting helped a lot when I took tests and when I studied. After looking at the coursework for the rest of the college major I decided to switch to that major. I graduated with a much better GPA in that field and it opened up more possibilities for me after graduation."—a college graduate with ADHD

Social and Emotional Considerations

It has been reported that students with ADHD are more prone to depression symptoms than other students.[4] This means that taking care of your mental health is an important part of going to college. Taking care of your own mental health may not be something that you thought about so much before college. Maybe this was something that your parents thought about more than you did. However, as you get older it is more and more your own responsibility.

No one knows you better than your friends and family; keeping in touch with them can help you to decide whether you are too stressed, too down, angry, or frustrated. Keep in touch with your family and set limits on social activities and substance use. Make sure that you are getting sleep and eating properly. It is possible to thrive in college with or without ADHD.

Maybe it took years to build your social connections in high school. In college you have to start all over again. Most schools offer campus counseling or support groups. In addition, your health insurance may also cover mental health treatment such as counseling, which can also be useful for healthy emotional functioning.

Risk-Taking Behaviors

Risk-taking behaviors can be defined as "any consciously, or non-consciously controlled behavior with a perceived uncertainty about its outcome, and/or about its possible benefits, or costs for the physical, economic or psycho-social well-being of oneself or others."[5] Risk-taking behaviors appears in this chapter because there are some special warnings for students with ADHD who are entering college. All of the information included in this book is meant to give you the knowledge and tools to allow you to thrive. Imagine if you were driving down the street and you saw a sign that said caution or danger; the sign isn't meant to scare you but rather to give you fair warning that there is something that you should pay attention to up ahead. This section is no different. Risk-taking behaviors can include the following:

- Cigarettes or tobacco products
- Illegal drugs
- Prescription medications
- Alcohol consumption
- Risky sexual activity
- Fighting
- Climbing
- Impulsive spending
- Speeding or unsafe driving
- Inappropriate social behavior

Risk-taking behaviors may be more likely to happen in environments with little supervision; increased access to substances like alcohol or illegal or prescription drugs; or people under the influence of alcohol or drugs. In addition, risk-taking behaviors can also be increased by impulsiveness. When all of these factors are mixed together, it can lead to negative results.

Remember when risk taking, you may not know the outcome. Spending a lot of money on a new computer is OK if you have budgeted for it and you know you have the money. Impulsively buying a large-ticket item on a whim, after a night of partying, without checking your bank account, is a bad idea. In addition, if you are in an environment where risk-taking behaviors are accepted then there are less social consequences for your actions.

Risk-taking behaviors can include those that can have big consequences and almost no benefits. Can you think of a behavior that can have very negative consequences and almost no benefits? © iStock / marrio31

Did you know that individuals with ADHD have higher rates of smoking?[6] In addition, only a few people with ADHD are able to quit smoking once they have started.[7] The consequences of smoking are increased health risks including heart disease, cardiovascular disease, and cancer. The best strategy is not to start.

College students with ADHD have been reported to have a higher rate of problematic alcohol consumption. Binge drinking is a form of problematic alco-

Potential Consequences of Risk-Taking Behaviors

- Physical injury
- Poor health
- Poor grades
- Low credit score
- Fines
- Incarceration
- Criminal record
- Sexually transmitted diseases
- Unplanned pregnancies
- Inappropriate material posted on the Internet

hol consumption that is defined as four drinks for women and five for men in less than a two-hour period.[8] The consequences of binge drinking can include risky sexual behavior, injuries, car accidents, trouble with the law, and much more.

The use of alcohol or drugs can impair your ability to make good decisions, which can put you at risk for many problems. Risky sexual behavior is a problem that can include having multiple sexual partners and not practicing safe sex. It can result in unplanned pregnancies and an increased risk of getting a sexually transmitted illness.

Other risk-taking behaviors such as fighting, speeding, and climbing when not appropriate are known to be higher in individuals with ADHD and can result in both physical injury and trouble with the law.

Risk-taking behaviors can start as poor coping skills for anxiety, frustration, lack of purpose, or excitement but can turn into bad habits. The earlier in life you start bad habits, the harder they are to break. Luckily, the earlier you start good habits, the harder they are to break as well. Start good habits early and crowd out the time for the bad ones:

- Instead of speeding, buy a car that can't go fast.
- Instead of partying hard, hang out with friends who don't drink or who drink responsibly.
- Instead of playing a dangerous sport, play a sport that requires you to stay fit and keep in shape.
- Instead of smoking, lift weights or jog to feel more relaxed.
- Instead of overeating to deal with stress, play a musical instrument.
- Instead of seeking out relationships that are exciting, build relationships that are stable.
- Instead of fulfilling the urge for excitement in uncontrolled environments, get it in environments that are safe, such as rock climbing at an indoor facility with a harness.
- Instead of gambling online, join a fantasy sports league with friends or play video games.
- Instead of going to a sports bar every night, go for a nightly walk with a friend.

Many people have described a certain restlessness that comes with ADHD. Finding positive ways to address this restlessness can start when you are in college and can have positive effects for the rest of your life.

It is worth saying that self-management, academics, social and emotional considerations, and risk-taking behaviors can all have an impact on each other. In other words, only worrying about one of these areas is not enough; you need to manage all of them. For example, only worrying about grades may get you good grades in the moment, but it will have a negative effect on the other areas, such as social functioning and self-management. Likewise, only worrying about the social aspects of college will most likely have negative effects on your grades. Striving for a balanced lifestyle will have a positive effect on your social, emotional, and academic functioning. This positive effect will help you make better decisions, have stability, and enjoy greater success in the long run.

Career

Did you know that the average American could spend a third of his life at work? It's true, so it is important to choose something that you enjoy and makes you feel good. So, you may be wondering, "What do I want to be when I grow up?" If you are still in high school this may seem like a million miles away, but it is something that everyone thinks about. Maybe you want to be a policeman or a fireman, or maybe you want to work in business or finance, or maybe you want to go into education or sports. The number of options you have is limitless. Should you be wondering about ADHD when you pick a profession. The answer could be yes and no. There is a famous quote that goes "whether you think you can do something or you can't, you are probably right." As you learned in chapter 10, many successful people in lots of different professions have ADHD, and as you learned in chapter 9 people with ADHD have many gifts in addition to the difficulties. Picking a career involves thinking about not only what you can or can't do but what you want to do. There is another expression that goes, "If you pick a job you love, you will never have to work a day in your life."

According to some research, people with ADHD have higher rates of unemployment than the general population.[9] In addition it has been reported that people with ADHD have lower than average household income, more workers compensation, and injury claims. It was reported by the World Health Organization that people with ADHD are absent more days a year than other employees and also have decreased work performance more often.[10] This has led to research about negative effects of ADHD in the workplace and the cost to the US economy.

This does not mean that people with ADHD are lazy or stupid or even that they do not like their jobs. It means that people with ADHD may have extra challenges that others do not have. If you realize these challenges and prepare for them, things can be a lot easier. However, simply getting the job done is not enough. Some people with untreated ADHD must work harder to get their job done in the same amount of time. For some this may feel like not being able to perform your job effectively, getting frustrated, and quitting. For others it may involve working extra hours to complete the same amount of work that everyone else can do within the workday. Carrying this extra load can weigh heavily after a while and eventually lead to burnout and decreased work performance. Having a plan to manage ADHD can help lighten the load and make things easier.

When choosing a career everyone has to look at their gifts and skills. What do you like to do and what do you not like to do? What are your capabilities? Choosing a career when you have ADHD is no different than choosing a career if you don't. Everyone has their own likes, dislikes, skills, and gifts. ADHD is no different, although you might want to keep in mind the following considerations that are specific to ADHD:

- If you are physically restless, you may not want to do a job that requires you to sit all day. Instead you may want to choose a job where you can freely move from place to place.
- If you are bored easily, you may not want to do a job that is predictable and always the same. Instead you may want to choose a job that frequently exposes you to new experiences, places, and people.
- If you are creative you may not want a job that requires you to do the same thing all the time. Instead you may want to choose a job that requires you to problem solve.
- If you do not like to do long-term planning, you may not want to choose a job that requires you to be very precise with planning. Instead you may want to choose a job that focuses on the task at hand and focuses on short-term goals and results.
- If you have a hard time with organization, you may not want to choose a job that requires you to pay attention to every little detail. Instead you may want to choose a job that requires you to look at the bigger picture.
- If you have a hard time writing a lot, you may not want to choose a job that is primarily based on writing. Instead you may want to choose a job that requires you to talk and interact with people.
- If you have a hard time staying organized, you may not want to choose a job that requires you to keep your own schedule. Instead you may want to choose a job that provides a highly structured schedule for you.[11]

You may be wondering why college and career are discussed in the same chapter and also why you would think about what you want to do when you grow up now, when you are still a teenager. Thinking about what you like to do can never start too early. Your hobbies and likes in high school may help you chose a college major, your college major will link to your career choice, and your career choice will be a very important part of your life. Thinking about the area you would like to study and work in is just as important as thinking about the type of job you would like to have in that area.

But job planning does not just start after college. Many young people have jobs in high school and college: part-time jobs, internships, volunteer experiences, and more. These are excellent opportunities to discover other aspects of

Career Choices

Richard, a car salesman said, "For me sales was the way to go. I have always had great people skills and I like to talk. I found that the challenge of selling cars was the right job for me. I could walk around, talk to people and I was good at knowing what the customers wanted. Eventually I was such a good salesman I became a manager for the dealership."

Barbara works in business and says, "I work from home. Working from home is an excellent option for me because being tied down to a desk and a 9–5 job is just not for me. Working from home allows me to start when I want and work at my own pace. If I want to eat lunch or take breaks, I can."

work, for example, do you like having a boss or would you like to work on your own? Would you like to work for a company or start your own business? Do you like to work outside or inside? Do you like to interact with people all day as part of a team or work by yourself? Do you like to work with children or adults or maybe older people? Would you like to work in a retail or sales environment or something corporate? How would you like to dress for work: dressed up or casual? Do you want to work in finance or education? Do you want to make a social impact or are you more interested in business? These are all questions you can begin to ask yourself when you are young.

Let's think about the example of an NBA basketball player and a thoroughbred jockey. Both are professional athletes, both can be champions; however the average height of a jockey is five feet two inches and the average height of an NBA basketball player is six feet seven inches. Although not impossible, it would be very difficult for a champion basketball player to be a champion jockey, and it would be equally difficult for a champion jockey to be a champion basketball player, because of their weight and height. This is not meant to discourage you from picking a career. It's only meant to illustrate that you must look at the requirements for a career or major. If you are willing to work hard, to make it work, then do it. If you do not love the career that much and are not willing to put the work in, then pick something else.

Having ADHD should not dictate what you do when you grow up, but you may want to think of it as a guiding principle. For example, you may like to take mechanical objects apart and put them back together but you may not want to consider working for a company on an assembly line where you have to spend long uninterrupted periods doing the same thing and sitting/standing in the same place. Being a mechanic may be more your speed where you can move freely, problem solve, make your own hours, and own your own business. There is nothing that you cannot do, but there may be lots of things you don't want to do. Maybe you like to drive but being a truck driver and spending long uninterrupted hours driving seems boring for you. Maybe being a UPS delivery driver is more your speed, allowing you to drive, stop, and empty your truck all day.

Adults with ADHD are eligible for accommodations in their workplace or educational settings under the Americans with Disabilities Act. The severity of their ADHD must produce impairments in one or more major areas of life functioning. To receive the accommodations, you must also disclose your disorder to your employer or educational institution. [12] This can be very helpful if disclosed to an educational institution. However, some employers may not understand ADHD and it may not be best to disclose. The best accommodation for your job could be choosing a job that you do not need accommodations for. Remember if you work better under certain conditions such as those stated earlier in the chapter, simply tell your employer that you work better under those conditions and see if they will change your job responsibilities to match.

School and career will most likely play a large role in your life for years to come. Everyone is different, but it is worth thinking about how ADHD will have an impact on your school life and eventually your career to ensure that you have a successful experience.

"After college I had a few jobs that I was not really good at and did not like. I spent time doing construction and also working as a waiter. Finally, I decided that I would like to go back to school and become a teacher. I enrolled in an alternate route program that would allow me to be a teacher while finishing my classes at night. I was never a great student but the classes were manageable. I am so glad that I began teaching, it is one of the hardest jobs that I have ever done but so rewarding. As a person with ADHD I found that the schedule was helpful, I had to work on the same schedule as the kids, the bell rang and my class left and the next class came in. The structure of the job was helpful for me. During class I could walk around the room and lecture about American history, a topic that I love to read about and study. Having class participation allowed me and the students to stay engaged in the material. The more difficult part of the job was reading and grading papers but overall it is a good fit for me. I also have an opportunity to instill the love of learning in students and help students that are having a hard time in school."—adult teacher with ADHD

Glossary

accommodation   a change in the timing, formatting, setting, scheduling, or presenting of an assignment in order to level the playing field in a classroom

anatomy   the structure of something, or how it is built

attention-deficit/hyperactivity disorder (ADHD)   a neurodevelopmental disorder that causes symptoms such as hyperactivity, inattention, and impulsivity

bullying   aggressive, unwanted, repetitive behavior intended to harm, intimidate, or humiliate another

combined presentation   a type of ADHD in which one demonstrates symptoms of inattention, hyperactivity, and impulsivity

confidentiality   a term referring to the responsibility of doctors, counselors, therapists, and so on to keep one's medical information private; rules of confidentiality vary based on the patient's age, location, and reason for visiting

cyberbullying   bullying that occurs over some form of electronic communication to harass, intimidate, spread rumors, impersonate, or exclude someone

diagnosis   the result of a doctor examining a patient's symptoms, behaviors, and patterns and determining what is wrong

disorder   a problem that causes a lack of functioning in an area of your life

emotional impulsivity   a symptom of ADHD in which one often reacts emotionally to a situation without thinking it through

executive functions   a group of thought processes that people with ADHD often struggle with

gifted   a term used to describe youth who give evidence of high achievement capability and who need services and activities not ordinarily provided by schools in order to develop those capabilities

hyperactivity   a symptom of ADHD in which one has trouble sitting still

hyperfocus   a phenomenon in which one is able to be incredibly engaged in a particular activity for an extended period of time

imagination network   the aspect of the brain involved in constructing mental images in order to remember past events, think about the future, and imagine alternate perspectives and scenarios

impulsivity   a symptom of ADHD in which one does not think things through before doing or saying them

inattention   a symptom of ADHD in which one has trouble focusing attention or becomes easily distracted

incidence   the number of new ADHD diagnoses in a period of time

inhibition   the ability to prevent thoughts and actions that are inappropriate for a situation; one of the seven primary executive functions

modification   a change in an assignment that lowers or reduces the expectation in some way

neurodevelopmental delay   a slowing in the process of one's brain development

organizing   the ability to put things in order to help with the completion of tasks; one of the seven primary executive functions

planning and goal setting   the ability to think through a task and to make plans, set reasonable goals, and solve problems; one of the seven primary executive functions

predominantly hyperactive–impulsive presentation   a type of ADHD in which one demonstrates symptoms mostly of hyperactivity and impulsivity

predominantly inattentive presentation   a type of ADHD in which one demonstrates symptoms mostly of inattention

prevalence   the total number of people with ADHD in a population

prioritizing   the ability to recognize which components of tasks are the most important and to focus on relevant details; one of the seven primary executive functions

processing speed   the ability of the human brain to take in and analyze a lot of information in a short period of time

self-concept   the thoughts and feelings that one has about one's own self

self-regulation   the ability to regulate one's behavior and monitor one's own thoughts and actions; one of the seven primary executive functions

shifting   the ability to devise new strategies and to be cognitively flexible when a situation changes

specific learning disability   a disorder in one or more of the basic psychological processes involved in understanding or using language, which may manifest itself in the imperfect ability to listen, think, speak, read, write, spell, or do mathematical calculations

working memory   the ability to hold and manipulate relevant information within one's mind; one of the seven primary executive functions

Notes

Chapter 1

1. "Data & Statistics," Centers for Disease Control and Prevention, 2016, www.cdc.gov/ ncbddd/adhd/data.html. Accessed June 26, 2016; American Psychiatric Association, *Diagnostic and Statistical Manual of Mental Disorders*, 5th ed. (*DSM-5*) (Washington, DC: American Psychiatric Association, 2013).
2. "Data & Statistics."
3. "Data & Statistics."
4. Jeffrey P. Brosco and Anna Bona, "Changes in Academic Demands and Attention-Deficit/ Hyperactivity Disorder in Young Children," *JAMA Pediatrics* 170, no. 4 (2016): 396. doi: 10.1001/jamapediatrics.2015.4132.
5. "Increasing ADHD Rates May Be Linked to Heightened Academic Expectations for Young Children," University of Miami Miller School of Medicine, med.miami.edu/news/ increasing-adhd-rates-may-be-linked-to-heightened-academic-expectations-for. Accessed June 29, 2016.
6. Vicky Anderson, Peter J. Anderson, Rani Jacobs, and Megan Spencer Smith, "Development and Assessment of Executive Functions: From Preschool to Adolescence," in *Executive Functions in the Frontal Lobes*, 123–54 (Philadelphia, PA: Taylor and Francis, 2008).
7. Anderson et al., "Development and Assessment of Executive Functions."
8. "Data & Statistics."
9. Barbara Franke, Stephen V Faraone, Philip Asherson, Jan Buitelaar, Claiton H Bau, Josep Antoni Ramos-Quiroga, Eric Mick, Eugenio H Grevet, Stefan Johansson, Jan Haavik, Klaus P Lesch, Bru Cormand, and Andreas Reif, "The Genetics of Attention Deficit/Hyperactivity Disorder in Adults, a Review," *Molecular Psychiatry* 17, no. 10 (2012): 960–87.
10. Franke et al., "The Genetics of Attention Deficit/Hyperactivity Disorder in Adults," 960–87.
11. American Psychiatric Association, *DSM-5*.
12. "IDEA—Building the Legacy of IDEA 2004." IDEA—Individuals with Disabilities Act, 2004, idea.ed.gov/explore/view/p/,root,statute,I,A,602,30,. Accessed June 26, 2016.
13. American Psychiatric Association, *DSM-5*.
14. American Psychiatric Association, *DSM-5*.
15. oicu8121983, "Russell Barkley—ADD, ODD, Emotional Impulsiveness, and Relationships," YouTube video published December 5, 2010, www.youtube.com/watch?v=rcwp9T3zNcM. Accessed January 1, 2018.
16. US Department of Education, "Title IX—General Provisions," www2.ed.gov/policy/elsec/ leg/esea02/pg107.html. Accessed June 29, 2016.
17. Jerome M. Sattler, *Foundations of Behavioral, Social and Clinical Assessment of Children*, 6th ed. (N.p.: Jerome M. Sattler Publishers, 2014).
18. Sattler, *Foundations of Behavioral, Social and Clinical Assessment of Children*; Mimi Wellisch and Jac Brown, "An Integrated Identification and Intervention Model for Intellectually Gifted Children," *Journal of Advanced Academics* 23, no. 2 (2012): 161–62. doi:10.1177/1932202x12438877.

19. Big Think, "How ADHD Affects Your Brain," YouTube video published 2011, www.you tube.com/watch?v=O8w0p4WCWiY. Accessed June 26, 2016.

---

a. Mona M. Shattell, Robin Bartlett, and Tracie Rowe, "'I Have Always Felt Different': The Experience of Attention-Deficit/Hyperactivity Disorder in Childhood," *Journal of Pediatric Nursing* 23, no. 1 (2008): 49–57, quote p. 53. doi:10.1016/j.pedn.2007.07.010.
b. American Psychiatric Association, *DSM-5*.
c. Shattell, Bartlett, and Rowe, "'I Have Always Felt Different,'" 52.

Chapter 2

1. American Psychiatric Association, *Diagnostic and Statistical Manual of Mental Disorders*, 3rd ed., rev. (*DSM-III-R*) (Washington, DC: American Psychiatric Association, 1987).
2. Office of the Historian, "Purchase of Alaska," Department of State, history.state.gov/mile stones/1866–1898/alaska-purchase. Accessed January 5, 2018.
3. "Concepts of Contagions and Epidemics," Harvard University Library, ocp.hul.harvard .edu/contagion/concepts.html. Accessed June 20, 2018.
4. Russell A. Barkley and Helmut Peters, "The Earliest Reference to ADHD in the Medical Literature? Melchior Adam Weikard's Description in 1775 of 'Attention Deficit'(Mangel der Aufmerksamkeit, Attentio Volubilis)," *Journal of Attention Disorders* 16, no. 8 (2012): 623–30.
5. Alexander Crichton, *An Inquiry into the Nature and Origin of Mental Derangement: Comprehending a Concise System of the Physiology and Pathology of the Human Mind* (London: Printed for T. Cadell, junior, and W. Davies, 1798).
6. George Frederic Still, *The Goulstonian Lectures on Some Abnormal Psychical Conditions in Children* (London: Lancet, 1902).
7. Franklin G. Ebaugh, "Neuropsychiatric Sequelae of Acute Epidemic Encephalitis in Children," *Archives of Pediatrics & Adolescent Medicine* 25, no. 2 (1923): 89. doi:10.1001/arch pedi.1923.01920020006002; "Timeline of ADHD Prevalence, Medications, and Diagnostic Criteria from 1990s to Current," Centers for Disease Control and Prevention, www.cdc.gov/ ncbddd/adhd/documents/timeline.pdf. Accessed June 20, 2018.
8. Klaus W. Lange, Susanne Reichl, Katharina M. Lange, Lara Tucha, and Oliver Tucha, "The History of Attention Deficit Hyperactivity Disorder," *ADHD Attention Deficit and Hyperactivity Disorders* 2, no. 4 (2010): 241–55. doi:10.1007/s12402-010-0045-8.
9. "Timeline of ADHD."
10. Lange et al., "The History of Attention Deficit Hyperactivity Disorder," 241–55.
11. Lange et al., "The History of Attention Deficit Hyperactivity Disorder," 241–55.
12. American Psychiatric Association, *DSM-III-R*.
13. "Ritalin Use among Youth: Examining the Issues and Concerns," Hearing before the Subcommittee on Early Childhood, Youth, and Families of the Committee on Education and the Workforce, US House of Representatives, 106th Congress, 2nd Session, May 16, 2000 (Washington, DC: Government Printing Office, 2000).
14. "Data & Statistics," Centers for Disease Control and Prevention, www.cdc.gov/ncbddd/adhd/ data.html. Accessed June 20, 2018.
15. Hearing: Ritalin Use among Youth: Examining the Issues and Concerns, Hearing before the Subcommittee on Early Childhood, Youth, and Families of the Committee on Education and

the Workforce, U.S. House of Representatives, 106th Congress, 2nd Session (16 May 2000). Washington, DC: Government Printing Office, 2000.

a. Heinrich Hoffmann, *Struwwelpeter: Merry Stories and Funny Pictures*, Project Gutenberg, www.gutenberg.org/files/12116/12116-h/12116-h.htm. Accessed June 20, 2018.
b. "Timeline of ADHD Prevalence, Medications, and Diagnostic Criteria from 1990s to Current," Centers for Disease Control and Prevention, www.cdc.gov/ncbddd/adhd/documents/timeline.pdf. Accessed June 20, 2018.
c. "Data & Statistics." https://www.cdc.gov/ncbddd/adhd/documents/timeline.pdf.

Chapter 3

1. "A 25 Year History of the IDEA," US Department of Education, www2.ed.gov/policy/speced/leg/idea/history.html. Accessed November 25, 2016.
2. "10 Facts about K–12 Funding," US Department of Education, www2.ed.gov/about/overview/fed/10facts/index.html?exp. Accessed November 25, 2016.
3. "An Overview of the Department of Education," US Department of Education, www2.ed.gov/about/overview/focus/what_pg2.html. Accessed November 25, 2016.
4. "The Federal Role in Education," US Department of Education, www2.ed.gov/about/overview/fed/role.html. Accessed November 25, 2016.
5. "Every Student Succeeds Act (ESSA)," US Department of Education, www.ed.gov/esea. Accessed November 25, 2016.
6. "Free and Appropriate Public Education for Students with Disabilities," US Department of Education, August 2010, www2.ed.gov/about/offices/list/ocr/docs/edlite-FAPE504.html. Accessed November 25, 2016.
7. "Attention Deficit Disorder (ADD/ADHD)," Wright's Law, www.wrightslaw.com/info/add.index.htm#sthash.6SlDSwko.dpuf. Accessed November 25, 2016.
8. "Family Rights and Privacy Act (FERPA)," US Department of Education, www2.ed.gov/policy/gen/guid/fpco/ferpa/index.html. Accessed November 25, 2016.
9. "A 25 Year History of the IDEA."
10. Office for Civil Rights, "Americans with Disabilities Act (ADA)," US Department of Education, www2.ed.gov/about/offices/list/ocr/docs/hq9805.html. Accessed November 25, 2016.
11. Office of Special Education and Rehabilitative Services, "Joint Policy Memorandum (ADD)," Wrights Law, www.wrightslaw.com/law/code_regs/OSEP_Memorandum_ADD_1991.html#sthash.akxYJtKb.dpuf. Accessed November 25, 2016.
12. United States Department of Education, "Memorandum," Wrights Law, www.wrightslaw.com/info/add.eval.ocrmemo.htm. Accessed June 26, 2018.
13. Office for Civil Rights, "Know Your Rights: Students with ADHD," US Department of Education, www2.ed.gov/about/offices/list/ocr/docs/dcl-know-rights-201607–504.pdf. Accessed November 25, 2016.
14. "A Guide to the Individualized Education Program," US Department of Education, www2.ed.gov/parents/needs/speced/iepguide/index.html. Accessed November 25, 2016.
15. "A Guide to the Individualized Education Program."

a. Arlene Sacks, *Special Education: A Reference Handbook* (Santa Barbara, CA: ABC-CLIO, 2001).

b. "Attention Deficit Disorder (ADD/ADHD)," Wright's Law, www.wrightslaw.com/info/add. index.htm#sthash.6SlDSwko.dpuf. Accessed November 25, 2016.

c. "Documents Related to *Brown v. Board of Education*," National Archives, www.archives.gov/ education/lessons/brown-v-board. Accessed November 25, 2016.

d. Family Educational Rights and Privacy Act (FERPA). 20 U.S.C. § 1232g; 34 CFR Part 99.

Chapter 4

1. Leslie Lundt, *You Can Think like a Psychiatrist: Understanding Psychiatric Medicines* (Eau Claire, WI: PESI, 2009).

2. Josh Constine, "Facebook Now Has 2 Billion Monthly Users . . . , and Responsibility," Tech Crunch, June 27, 2017, techcrunch.com/2017/06/27/facebook-2-billion-users/. Accessed January 15, 2018.

3. Steve Mazie, "Do You Have Too Many Facebook Friends?" Big Think, bigthink.com/praxis/ do-you-have-too-many-facebook-friends. Accessed January 15, 2018.

4. Greg Stuart, Nelson Spruston, and Michael Häusser, eds. *Dendrites* (Oxford: Oxford University Press, 2016).

5. Sylvester E. Vizi, A. Fekete, R. Karoly, and A. Mike, "Non-synaptic Receptors and Transporters Involved in Brain Functions and Targets of Drug Treatment," *British Journal of Pharmacology* 160, no. 4 (2010): 785–809.

6. John H. Martin, *Neuroanatomy Text and Atlas* (New York: McGraw-Hill Professional, 2012).

7. Stuart, Spruston, and Häusser, *Dendrites.*

8. Martin, *Neuroanatomy Text and Atlas.*

9. George Bartzokis, "Brain Myelination in Prevalent Neuropsychiatric Developmental Disorders: Primary and Comorbid Addiction," *Adolescent Psychiatry* 29 (2005): 55.

10. Tomáš Paus, Alex Zijdenbos, Keith Worsley, D. Louis Collins, Jonathan Blumenthal, Jay N. Giedd, Judith L. Rapoport, and Alan C. Evans, "Structural Maturation of Neural Pathways in Children and Adolescents: In Vivo Study." *Science* 283, no. 5409 (1999): 1908–11.

11. Benjamin R. Williams, Jonathan S. Ponesse, Russell J. Schachar, Gordon D. Logan, and Rosemary Tannock, "Development of Inhibitory Control across the Life Span," *Developmental Psychology* 35, no. 1 (1999): 205.

12. Anne-Claude Bedard, Shana Nichols, Jose A. Barbosa, Russell Schachar, Gordon D. Logan, and Rosemary Tannock, "The Development of Selective Inhibitory Control across the Life Span," *Developmental Neuropsychology* 21, no. 1 (2002): 93–111.

13. Sylvana Côté, Richard E. Tremblay, Daniel Nagin, Mark Zoccolillo, and Frank Vitaro, "The Development of Impulsivity, Fearfulness, and Helpfulness during Childhood: Patterns of Consistency and Change in the Trajectories of Boys and Girls," *Journal of Child Psychology and Psychiatry* 43, no. 5 (2002): 609–18.

14. Philip Shaw, K. Eckstrand, W. Sharp, J. Blumenthal, J. P. Lerch, D. E. E. A. Greenstein, L. Clasen, A. Evans, J. Giedd, and J. L. Rapoport, "Attention-Deficit/Hyperactivity Disorder Is Characterized by a Delay in Cortical Maturation," *Proceedings of the National Academy of Sciences* 104, no. 49 (2007): 19649–54.

15. Liz Neporent, "Missed ADHD Diagnosis, Lost Childhood," ABC News, March 11, 2014, abcnews.go.com/Health/missed-adhd-diagnosis-lost-childhood/story?id=22858720. Accessed March 1, 2018.

16. Z. Hawi, M. Dring, A. Kirley, D. Foley, L. Kent, N. Craddock, P. Asherson, et al., "Seroto-nergic System and Attention Deficit Hyperactivity Disorder (ADHD): A Potential Suscep-tibility Locus at the 5-HT 1B Receptor Gene in 273 Nuclear Families from a Multi-Centre Sample," *Molecular Psychiatry* 7, no. 7 (2002): 718.

17. Niklas Nordquist and Lars Oreland, "Serotonin, Genetic Variability, Behaviour, and Psychi-atric Disorders—a Review," *Upsala Journal of Medical Sciences* 115, no. 1 (2010): 2–10.

18. "The Serotonergic System," DNA Learning Center, www.dnalc.org/view/813-The-Seroto nergic-System.html. Accessed January 15, 2018.

19. Luca Passamonti, Molly J. Crockett, Annemieke M. Apergis-Schoute, Luke Clark, James B. Rowe, Andrew J. Calder, and Trevor W. Robbins, "Effects of Acute Tryptophan Depletion on Prefrontal-Amygdala Connectivity While Viewing Facial Signals of Aggression," *Biological Psychiatry* 71, no. 1 (2012): 36–43.

20. ADHD Videos, "30 Essential Ideas You Should Know about ADHD," YouTube video, pub-lished August 21, 2014, www.youtube.com/watch?v=G2u8E5UqEHU. Accessed March 1, 2018.

21. Kyle Menary, Paul F. Collins, James N. Porter, Ryan Muetzel, Elizabeth A. Olson, Vipin Kumar, Michael Steinbach, Kelvin O. Lim, and Monica Luciana, "Associations between Cor-tical Thickness and General Intelligence in Children, Adolescents and Young Adults," *Intel-ligence* 41, no. 5 (2013): 597–606.

22. Justin Remer, Elise Croteau-Chonka, Douglas C. Dean III, Sara D'arpino, Holly Dirks, Dan-nielle Whiley, and Sean C. L. Deoni, "Quantifying Cortical Development in Typically Devel-oping Toddlers and Young Children, 1–6 Years of Age," *NeuroImage* 153 (2017): 246–61.

23. Chandan J. Vaidya, "Neurodevelopmental Abnormalities in ADHD," in *Behavioral Neuro-science of Attention Deficit Hyperactivity Disorder and Its Treatment*, ed. Clare Stanford and Rosemary Tannock, pp. 49–66 (Berlin, Heidelberg, Germany: Springer, 2011).

24. Shaw et al., "Attention-Deficit/Hyperactivity Disorder Is Characterized," 19649–54.

25. Janos Kiss, Bernadett K. Szasz, Fodor László, Mike Arpad, Nora Lenkey, Dalma Kurkó, József Nagy, and E. Sylvester Vizi, "GluN2B-Containing NMDA Receptors as Possible Tar-gets for the Neuroprotective and Antidepressant Effects of Fluoxetine," *Neurochem Int* 60, no. 2 (2012):170–76.

26. jandkseminars, "Stimulants Protect ADHD Brains," YouTube video published May 17, 2015, www.youtube.com/watch?time_continue=158&v=HYq571cycqg. Accessed March 1, 2018.

27. TEDx Talks, "Drugs, Dopamine and Drosophila—A Fly Model for ADHD?" YouTube video published January 31, 2013, www.youtube.com/watch?v=L8Bd_p8pbQI. Accessed January 15, 2018.

28. "ADHD, DRD4, and Brain Development," DNA Learning Center, www.dnalc.org/view/2161-ADHD-DRD4-and-brain-development.html. Accessed January 1, 2018.

---

a. Shaw et al., "Attention-Deficit/Hyperactivity Disorder Is Characterized," 19649–54.

b. Humphrey P. Rang, *Rang and Dale's Pharmacology* (London: Churchill Livingstone Elsevier, 2007).

c. Martine Hoogman, Janita Bralten, Derrek P. Hibar, Maarten Mennes, Marcel P. Zwiers, Lizanne S. J. Schweren, Kimm J. E. van Hulzen, et al., "Subcortical Brain Volume Differ-ences in Participants with Attention Deficit Hyperactivity Disorder in Children and Adults: A Cross-Sectional Mega-Analysis," *Lancet Psychiatry* 4, no. 4 (2017): 310–19.

d. John H. Martin, *Neuroanatomy Text and Atlas* (New York: McGraw-Hill Professional, 2012).

e. TEDx Talks, "Drugs, Dopamine and Drosophila—A Fly Model for ADHD?" YouTube video published January 31, 2013, www.youtube.com/watch?v=L8Bd_p8pbQI. Accessed January 15, 2018.

Chapter 5

1. American Psychiatric Association, *Diagnostic and Statistical Manual of Mental Disorders*, 5th ed. (*DSM-5*) (Washington, DC: American Psychiatric Association, 2013).

2. Joshua Breslau, Elizabeth Miller, W-J. Joanie Chung, and Julie B. Schweitzer, "Childhood and Adolescent Onset Psychiatric Disorders, Substance Use, and Failure to Graduate High School on Time," *Journal of Psychiatric Research* 45, no. 3 (2011): 295–301.

3. Meta Hemenway-Forbes, "For ADHD Students, Transition to College Is Tough," *Courier*, September 1, 2013, wcfcourier.com/news/local/for-adhd-students-transition-to-college-is -tough/article_950df28a-ac05-5b50-8768-2ed34aa05376.html. Accessed June 1, 2017.

4. Andrea L. Green and David L. Rabiner, "What Do We Really Know about ADHD in College Students?" *Neurotherapeutics* 9, no. 3 (2012): 559–68.

5. Denis Brian, *The Unexpected Einstein: The Real Man behind the Icon* (Hoboken, NJ: John Wiley & Sons, 2005), 7.

6. Scott Barry Kaufman, "The Creative Gifts of ADHD," *Beautiful Minds* (*Scientific American* blog), October 21, 2014, blogs.scientificamerican.com/beautiful-minds/the-creative-gifts-of -adhd/. Accessed June 1, 2017.

7. Kaufman, "The Creative Gifts of ADHD."

8. Ruth Williams, "Sir John Gurdon: Godfather of Cloning," *Journal of Cell Biology* 181, no. 2 (2008): 178–79, www.ncbi.nlm.nih.gov/pmc/articles/PMC2315664/. Accessed June 1, 2017.

9. Peter Wright, "School Accommodations and Modifications,"Wright's Law, www.wrightslaw .com/info/sec504.accoms.mods.pdf. Accessed June 1, 2017.

10. Wright, "School Accommodations and Modifications."

11. Russell A. Barkley, "Classroom Accommodations for Children with ADHD," *ADHD Report* 16, no. 4 (2008): 7–10.

12. Stephen T. Peverly, Pooja C. Vekaria, Lindsay A. Reddington, James F. Sumowski, Kamauru R. Johnson, and Crystal M. Ramsay, "The Relationship of Handwriting Speed, Working Memory, Language Comprehension and Outlines to Lecture Note-Taking and Test-Taking among College Students," *Applied Cognitive Psychology* 27, no. 1 (2013): 115–26.

13. Peverly et al., "The Relationship of Handwriting Speed," 115–26.

14. Russell Barkley, *Attention-Deficit Hyperactivity Disorder: A Handbook for Diagnosis and Treatment*, 3rd ed. (New York: Guilford Press, 2014).

15. Angela Duckworth, "The Key to Success? Grit," TED, www.ted.com/talks/angela_lee_duck worth_grit_the_power_of_passion_and_perseverance. Accessed March 14, 2016.

16. "The Teen Brain: 6 Things to Know," National Institute of Mental Health, www.nimh.nih.gov/ health/publications/the-teen-brain-6-things-to-know/index.shtml. Accessed June 1, 2017.

17. Katya Trudeau Potkin and William E. Bunney Jr., "Sleep Improves Memory: The Effect of Sleep on Long Term Memory in Early Adolescence," *PLoS One* 7, no. 8 (2012): e42191.

18. Penny Corkum, Rosemary Tannock, and Harvey Moldofsky. "Sleep Disturbances in Children with Attention-Deficit/Hyperactivity Disorder," *Journal of the American Academy of Child & Adolescent Psychiatry* 37, no. 6 (1998): 637–46.

19. "Procrastination," Albert Ellis Institute, albertellis.org/procrastination/. Accessed September 1, 2017.

---

a. Kathy Crockett, "Jay Leno, Comedian and Television Personality," Yale Center for Dyslexia and Creativity, dyslexia.yale.edu/leno.html. Accessed June 1, 2017.
b. "Most Decks of Playing Cards Memorized—Single Sighting," Guinness World Records, www.guinnessworldrecords.com/world-records/most-decks-of-playing-cards-memorized -single-sighting. Accessed June 1, 2017.

Chapter 6

1. John Branch, "No Dribbling and No Passing, but Free Throws Are Nonstop," *New York Times*, March 14, 2012, www.nytimes.com/2012/03/15/sports/ncaabasketball/free-throw -records-fall-with-the-flick-of-his-wrist.html. Accessed January 1, 2018.
2. Edward Hallowell, "Avoid the S.P.I.N. Cycle of ADHD," Dr. Hallowell.com, http://www .drhallowell.com/avoid-the-s-p-i-n-cycle-of-adhd/. Accessed January 1, 2018.
3. "Not Just Living but Thriving with ADHD," TEDx Talks, YouTube video published June 8, 2017, www.youtube.com/watch?v=I0DLQ8MUgTk. Accessed January 15, 2018.
4. "It Took Me a Long Time," ADHD Awareness Month, October 1, 2014, www.adhdaware nessmonth.org/it-took-me-a-long-time. Accessed January 1, 2018.
5. "Data & Statistics," Centers for Disease Control and Prevention, www.cdc.gov/ncbddd/adhd/ data.html. Accessed January 1, 2018.

---

a. Albert Ellis and Michael E. Bernard, eds. *Rational Emotive Behavioral Approaches to Childhood Disorders: Theory, Practice and Research.* Springer Science & Business Media, 2006.
b. Lynn McKeague, Eilis Hennessy, Claire O'Driscoll, and Caroline Heary, "Retrospective Accounts of Self-Stigma Experienced by Young People with Attention-Deficit/Hyperactivity Disorder (ADHD) or Depression," *Psychiatric Rehabilitation Journal* 38, no. 2 (2015): 158.
c. "Simone Biles," ESPN.com, September 21, 2016, www.espn.com/espnw/voices/article/ 17602540/bravo-simone-biles-taking-stand-adhd-stigma. Accessed January 1, 2018.
d. "The Stars Who Aligned ADHD with Success," ADDitude, www.additudemag.com/suc cessful-people-with-adhd-learning-disabilities/. Accessed January 1, 2018.

Chapter 7

1. "Protecting Your Privacy: Understanding Confidentiality," American Psychological Association, www.apa.org/helpcenter/confidentiality.aspx. Accessed January 15, 2018.
2. "Protecting Your Privacy."
3. "Attention Deficit Hyperactivity Disorder," National Institute of Mental Health, www.nimh .nih.gov/health/topics/attention-deficit-hyperactivity-disorder-adhd/index.shtml. Accessed January 20, 2018.
4. "What Is ADHD?" American Psychiatric Association, www.psychiatry.org/patients-fami lies/adhd/what-is-adhd. Accessed January 20, 2018.
5. "My Child Has Been Diagnosed with ADHD—Now What?" Centers for Disease Control, www.cdc.gov/ncbddd/adhd/treatment.html. Accessed January 20, 2018.

6. American Academy of Pediatrics, "Clinical Practice Guideline: Treatment of the School-Aged Child with Attention-Deficit/Hyperactivity Disorder, *Pediatrics* 108, no. 4 (2001), pediatrics.aappublications.org/content/108/4/1033. Accessed January 20, 2018.

7. Editors of *ADDitude, A Parent's Guide to ADHD Medication* (New York: New Hope Media, 2017), www.additudemag.com/wp-content/uploads/2017/05/A-Parents-Guide-to-ADHD-Medications-5.pdf. Accessed January 15, 2018.

8. Dr. Hallowell, "Letter to the *New York Times*," Hallowell NYC, December 5, 2012, www.hallowellnyc.com/HallowellNYC/Blog/Archives/index.cfm?objectType=article&objectID=31084. Accessed June 28, 2018.

9. "Drug Scheduling," Drug Enforcement Administration, www.dea.gov/druginfo/ds.shtml. Accessed January 15, 2018.

10. "Drug Scheduling."

a. New York State Office of Mental Health, "Attention Deficit Hyperactivity Disorder," https://www.omh.ny.gov/omhweb/booklets/adhd.pdf. Accessed January 15, 2018. Child Mind Institute, "Side Effects of ADHD Medication," https://childmind.org/article/side-effects-of-adhd-medication/. Accessed January 15, 2018.

Chapter 8

1. Bella DePaulo, "What Is the Divorce Rate Really?" *Psychology Today*, February 2, 2017, www.psychologytoday.com/blog/living-single/201702/what-is-the-divorce-rate-really. Accessed January 20, 2018.

2. Jonathan Vespa, Jamie M. Lewis, and Rose M. Kreider, "America's Families and Living Arrangements," United States Census, www.census.gov/prod/2013pubs/p20-570.pdf. Accessed January 20, 2018.

3. Susan M. McHale, Kimberly A. Updegraff, and Shawn D. Whiteman, "Sibling Relationships and Influences in Childhood and Adolescence," *Journal of Marriage and Family* 74, no. 5 (2012): 913–30.

4. McHale, Updegraff, and Whiteman. "Sibling Relationships," 913–30.

5. Anita Thapar and Evangelia Stergiakouli, "An Overview on the Genetics of ADHD," *Xin li xue bao. Acta psychologica Sinica* 40, no. 10 (2008): 1088.

6. Thapar and Stergiakouli, "An Overview on the Genetics of ADHD," 1088.

7. Thapar and Stergiakouli, "An Overview on the Genetics of ADHD," 1088.

8. Kerry King, Daleen Alexander, and Joseph Seabi, "Siblings' Perceptions of Their ADHD-Diagnosed Sibling's Impact on the Family System," *International Journal of Environmental Research and Public Health* 13, no. 9 (2016): 910.

9. King, Alexander, and Seabi, "Siblings' Perceptions," 910.

10. King, Alexander, and Seabi, "Siblings' Perceptions," 910.

11. King, Alexander, and Seabi, "Siblings' Perceptions," 910.

12. Dennis R. Trinidad, Chih-Ping Chou, Jennifer B. Unger, C. Anderson Johnson, and Yan Li, "Family Harmony as a Protective Factor against Adolescent Tobacco and Alcohol Use in Wuhan, China," *Substance Use & Misuse* 38, no. 8 (2003): 1159–71; Xianming Carroll du Prel, Honggang Yi, Yuezhu Liang, Ke Pang, Sandra Leeper-Woodford, Patrizia Riccardi, and Xianhong Liang, "Family-Environmental Factors Associated with Attention Deficit Hyperactivity Disorder in Chinese Children: A Case-Control Study," *PLoS One* 7, no. 11 (2012): e50543.

13. Valerie A. Harpin, "The Effect of ADHD on the Life of an Individual, Their Family, and Community from Preschool to Adult Life," *Archives of Disease in Childhood* 90, suppl. no. 1 (2005): i2–i7.

a. "Category: ADHD Stories," ADHD Awareness Month, October 22, 2016, www.adhdaware nessmonth.org/category/stories/. Accessed January 20, 2018.
b. TEDx Talks, "ADHD Sucks, but Not Really: Salif Mahamane: TEDxUSU," YouTube video published December 18, 2015, www.youtube.com/watch?v=fWCocjh5aK0I. Accessed January 20, 2018.
c. "Category: ADHD Stories."

Chapter 9

1. Karen Sampson Hoffman and Pamela Mercer, "When Dr. Barkley met Dr. Hallowell," ADHD: Neither Gift nor Curse, www.chadd.org/AttentionPDFs/ATTN_02_12_NeitherGift NorCurse.pdf. Accessed September 1, 2017.
2. Child Mind Institute, "Dr. Edward (Ned) Hallowell on ADHD: A Ferrari in Your Brain," YouTube video published June 7, 2011, www.youtube.com/watch?v=i5D56Cg7y4I. Accessed September 1, 2017.
3. The Official Licensing Site of Albert Einstein, einstein.biz/#quotations. Accessed September 1, 2017.
4. Scott Barry Kaufman, "The Creative Gifts of ADHD," *Beautiful Minds* (*Scientific American* blog), October 21, 2014, blogs.scientificamerican.com/beautiful-minds/the-creative-gifts-of -adhd/. Accessed September 1, 2017.
5. Scott Barry Kaufman, "The Real Neuroscience of Creativity," *Beautiful Minds* (*Scientific American* blog), August 19, 2013, blogs.scientificamerican.com/beautiful-minds/the-real -neuroscience-of-creativity/. Accessed September 1, 2017.
6. TEDx Talks, "ADHD Sucks, but Not Really: Salif Mahamane: TEDxUSU," YouTube video published December 18, 2015, www.youtube.com/watch?v=fWCocjh5aK0I. Accessed January 15, 2018.
7. *Airplane!* Directed by Jim Abrahams, David Zucker, and Jerry Zucker. Paramount, 1980.
8. Kaufman, "The Creative Gifts of ADHD."
9. TEDx Talks, "Living with ADHD in the Age of Information and Social Media: Theo Siggelakis: TEDxQuinnipiacU," YouTube video published July 3, 2014, www.youtube.com/ watch?v=y0hY5TYVv_s. Accessed January 15, 2018.
10. Mihaly Csikszentmihalyi, ""Flow, the Secret to Happiness," TED video published 2004, www.ted.com/talks/mihaly_csikszentmihalyi_on_flow. Accessed June 24, 2018.
11. Jonathan Williams and Eric Taylor, "The Evolution of Hyperactivity, Impulsivity and Cognitive Diversity," *Journal of the Royal Society Interface* 3, no. 8 (2006): 399–413.
12. Marc Lewis, "Disease, Disorder, or Neurodiversity: The Case of ADHD," *Psychology Today*, May 21, 2012, www.psychologytoday.com/blog/addicted-brains/201205/disease-disorder-or -neurodiversity-the-case-adhd. Accessed January 15, 2018.
13. Don Baker, "Neurodiversity and ADHD: In Support of Divergent Thinking," Unpacking ADHD, February 17, 2016, www.unpackingadhd.com/neurodiversity-and-adhd-in-support -of-divergent-thinking/. Accessed January 15, 2018.

14. Marthe S. Thagaard, Stephen V. Faraone, Edmund J. Sonuga-Barke, and Søren D. Øster-gaard, "Empirical Tests of Natural Selection-Based Evolutionary Accounts of ADHD: A Systematic Review," *Acta Neuropsychiatrica* 28, no. 5 (2016): 249–56.

15. Dan T. A. Eisenberg, Benjamin Campbell, Peter B. Gray, and Michael D. Sorenson, "Dopamine Receptor Genetic Polymorphisms and Body Composition in Undernourished Pastoralists: An Exploration of Nutrition Indices among Nomadic and Recently Settled Ariaal Men of Northern Kenya," *BMC Evolutionary Biology* 8, no. 1 (2008): 173.

16. Nur Cayirdag and Selcuk Acar, "Relationship between Styles of Humor and Divergent Thinking," *Procedia-Social and Behavioral Sciences* 2, no. 2 (2010): 3236–40.

17. New Jersey 101.5, "Sinbad Defends ADHD/ADD," YouTube video published June 29, 2017, www.youtube.com/watch?v=BwpVv5iYBCI. Accessed January 15, 2018.

18. BBC 5 Live, "Comedian Rory Bremner: Living with ADHD Is 'Hell,'" YouTube video published October 28, 2014, www.youtube.com/watch?v=_gRfuCIjafE. Accessed January 15, 2018.

19. Jeff Nichols, *Trainwreck: My Life as an Idiot* (New York: Touchstone, 2007), summary by Douglas Cootey, *ADDitude*, www.additudemag.com/trainwreck-my-life-as-an-idiot/. Accessed January 15, 2018.

20. Grace Friedman, "Peer Mentoring—Strengthening the ADHD Community," *The Blog* (*Huffington Post*), www.huffingtonpost.com/grace-friedman/peer-mentoring-strengthen_b_11156854.html. Accessed January 15, 2018.

21. Paul Caldarella, Robert Jeff Gomm, Ryan H. Shatzer, and D. Gary Wall, "School-Based Mentoring: A Study of Volunteer Motivations and Benefits," *International Electronic Journal of Elementary Education* 2, no. 2 (2010): 199–216.

22. Student Affairs Administrators in Higher Education, "Lehigh University Peer Mentor Program for Students with Learning Disabilities," www.naspa.org/images/uploads/main/Bronze1179.pdf. Accessed January 15, 2018.

a. Tiffany Bentley, "Awolnation Frontman Aaron Bruno Explains Dark Song Themes Mixed with Positive Beats," *Express Times*, November 23, 2011, www.lehighvalleylive.com/music/index.ssf/2011/11/awolnation_frontman_aaron_brun.html. Accessed September 1, 2017.

b. TEDx Talks, "Living with ADHD in the Age of Information and Social Media: Theo Siggelakis: TEDxQuinnipiacU," YouTube video published July 3, 2014, www.youtube.com/watch?v=y0hY5TYVv_s. Accessed January 15, 2018.

Chapter 10

1. Reading Rockets, "Dave Pilkey's Message to Kids with Learning Differences," YouTube video published October 2, 2017, www.youtube.com/watch?v=0xoIW6hXXk0. Accessed January 1, 2018.

2. Reading Rockets, "Dave Pilkey's Message."

3. Reading Rockets, "Dave Pilkey's Message."

4. Alonzo Delung, "Running Wild with Bear Grylls S01E03 Channing Tatum," YouTube video published April 6, 2017, www.youtube.com/watch?v=1Swzb4p1DpM. Accessed January 1, 2018.

5. Child Mind Institute, "Michael Phelps #My Younger Self," YouTube video published May 9, 2017, www.youtube.com/watch?v=XGynNTwUq3Y. Accessed January 1, 2018.

6. Child Mind Institute, "Michael Phelps #My Younger Self."

7. Understood, "Simone Biles on ADHD: Uplifting Words of Advice," YouTube video published October 12, 2017, www.youtube.com/watch?v=KbYSNww979g. Accessed January 1, 2018.
8. TotallyADD, "Greg LeMond on Having ADHD," YouTube video published March 27, 2012, www.youtube.com/watch?v=UWA839CN8Bg. Accessed January 1, 2018.
9. TotallyADD, "Greg LeMond on Having ADHD."
10. VeloNews.com, "Must Hear: Greg LeMond Speaks Out in Wide-Ranging Interview on Irish Radio," VeloNews, October 6, 2012, www.velonews.com/2012/10/news/must-hear-greg -lemond-speaks-out-in-wide-ranging-interview-on-irish-radio_256161#JxAwIEhJLEBbS 1Eg.99. Accessed January 1, 2018
11. OWN, "Lisa Gets Her Test Results: Our America with Lisa Ling: Oprah Winfrey Network," YouTube video, June 12, 2014, www.youtube.com/watch?v=YC9weSLoyrw. Accessed January 1, 2018.
12. Adam Levine, "Maroon 5's Adam Levine: 'ADHD Isn't a Bad Thing,'" *ADDitutde*, www .additudemag.com/adam-levine-adhd-is-not-a-bad-thing-and-you-are-not-alone/. Accessed January 1, 2018.
13. Elite Daily, "Elite Interviews David Neeleman, Founder of Jet and Aviation Entrepreneur," YouTube video published April 1, 2013, www.youtube.com/watch?v=QybWxHdiSpk&t=317s. Accessed January 1, 2018.
14. Elite Daily, "Elite Interviews David Neeleman."
15. ADHD Richmond, "Astronaut Scott Kelly Talks about His ADHD," YouTube video published November 23, 2017, www.youtube.com/watch?v=OoWjeLVBMzg. Accessed January 1, 2018.
16. OWN, "Music as Medicine: Visionaries: Inside the Creative Mind: Oprah Winfrey Network," YouTube video published November 6, 2011, www.youtube.com/watch?v=1zPepyTOXTI. Accessed January 1, 2018.
17. TEDx Talks, "I Have a Record-Breaking Memory—but Here's Why Forgetting May Save Humanity: Dave Farrow: TEDxUW," YouTube video published February 15, 2016, www .youtube.com/watch?v=7M5rFiVLeR0. Accessed January 1, 2018.
18. Alana Semuels, "Kinko's Founder All Shook Up as FedEx Drops the Name," *Money and Company* (*Los Angeles Times* blog), June 15, 2008, latimesblogs.latimes.com/money_co/2008/06/ post-2.html. Accessed January 1, 2018.
19. COC Cougar News, "Kinko's Founder Paul Orfelia Speaks at College of the Canyons," YouTube video published September 16, 2016, www.youtube.com/watch?v=LJAnr75Sjoo. Accessed January 1, 2018.
20. COC Cougar News, "Kinko's Founder Paul Orfelia Speaks."
21. Dr. Theresa Cerulli, "ADHD Live—Overview of Adult ADHD: Dr. Russell Barkley & Ty Pennington," YouTube video published January 9, 2014, www.youtube.com/watch ?v=B66nengrhZo. Accessed January 1, 2018.
22. Cerulli, "ADHD Live."
23. "The Glenn Beck Program," GlennBeck.com, July 22, 2008, www.glennbeck.com/content/ articles/article/196/12741/?utm_source=glennbeck&utm_medium=contentcopy_link. Accessed January 1, 2018.
24. "The Glenn Beck Program."
25. World Entertainment News Network, "Vaughn Glad His Dad Said No to Dyslexia Drugs," Con tactMusic.com, www.contactmusic.com/vince-vaughn/news/vaughn-glad-his-dad-said-no-to -dyslexia-drugs. Accessed January 1, 2018. "Vince Vaughn," University of Michigan, Dyslexia Help, dyslexiahelp.umich.edu/success-stories/vince-vaughn. Accessed January 1, 2018.

Chapter 11

1. Dewey Cornell and Susan P. Limber, "Law and Policy on the Concept of Bullying at School," *American Psychologist* 70, no. 4 (2015): 333.
2. "Other Types of Aggressive Behavior," StopBullying.gov, www.stopbullying.gov/what-is -bullying/other-types-of-aggressive-behavior/index.html. Accessed August 1, 2017.
3. "Other Types of Aggressive Behavior."
4. "Other Types of Aggressive Behavior."
5. Rick Albrecht, *Coaching Myths: Fifteen Wrong Ideas in Youth Sports* (Jefferson, NC: McFarland, 2013), 207.
6. "Other Types of Aggressive Behavior."
7. "Other Types of Aggressive Behavior."
8. Cornell and Limber, "Law and Policy," 333.
9. Erin Peebles, "Cyberbullying: Hiding behind the Screen," *Paediatrics & Child Health* 19, no. 10 (2014): 527–28.
10. New York State Senate, *Cyberbullying: A Report on Bullying in a Digital Age* (New York: Independent Democratic Congress, September 2011), www.nysenate.gov/sites/default/files/ final%20cyberbullying_report_september_2011_0_0.pdf. Accessed June 28, 2018.
11. "The Roles Kids Play in Bullying," StopBullying.gov, www.stopbullying.gov/what-is-bully ing/roles-kids-play/index.html. Accessed August 1, 2017.
12. National Center for Educational Statistics (NCES), *Student Reports of Bullying: Results from the 2015 School Crime Supplement to the National Crime Victimization Survey* (Washington, DC: US Department of Education, December 2016), T-1, nces.ed.gov/pubs2017/2017015. pdf. Accessed June 1, 2017.
13. NCES, *Student Reports of Bullying*, T-3.
14. NCES, *Student Reports of Bullying*, T-9.
15. NCES, *Student Reports of Bullying*, T-21.
16. Patricia McDougall and Tracy Vaillancourt, "Long-Term Adult Outcomes of Peer Victimization in Childhood and Adolescence: Pathways to Adjustment and Maladjustment," *American Psychologist* 70, no. 4 (2015): 300.
17. NCES, *Student Reports of Bullying*, T-27.
18. "Statistics," StopBullying.gov, www.stopbullying.gov/media/facts/index.html#stats. Accessed June 1, 2017.
19. "Who Is at Risk," StopBullying.gov, www.stopbullying.gov/at-risk/index.html. Accessed June 1, 2017.
20. Philip C. Rodkin, Dorothy L. Espelage, and Laura D. Hanish, "A Relational Framework for Understanding Bullying: Developmental Antecedents and Outcomes," *American Psychologist* 70, no. 4 (2015): 312.
21. "Warning Signs for Bullying," StopBullying.gov, www.stopbullying.gov/at-risk/warning -signs/index.html. Accessed June 1, 2017. Rodkin, Espelage, and Hanish, "A Relational Framework for Understanding Bullying," 311.
22. Kirstin Holmberg and Anders Hjern, "Bullying and Attention-Deficit–Hyperactivity Disorder in 10-Year-Olds in a Swedish Community," *Developmental Medicine & Child Neurology* 50, no. 2 (2008): 134–38; Linda Carroll, "Kids with ADHD May Be More Likely to Bully," NBCNews.com, January 29, 2008, www.nbcnews.com/id/22813400/ns/health -childrens_health/t/kids-adhd-may-be-more-likely-bully/#.WZSwGHeGNXQ. Accessed June 1, 2017.

23. "Key Components in State Anti-Bullying Laws," StopBullying.gov. www.stopbullying.gov/laws/key-components/index.html. Accessed June 1, 2017.

24. "Key Components in State Anti-Bullying Laws."

25. Shelley Hymel and Susan M. Swearer, "Four Decades of Research on School Bullying: An Introduction," *American Psychologist* 70, no. 4 (2015): 293.

26. Blake E. S. Taylor, *ADHD and Me: What I Learned from Lighting Fires at the Dinner Table* (Oakland, CA: New Harbinger Publications, 2008), 82.

27. McDougall and Vaillancourt, "Long-Term Adult Outcomes," 300.

Chapter 12

1. Joseph Biederman and Stephen V. Faraone, "The Effects of Attention-Deficit/Hyperactivity Disorder on Employment and Household Income," *Medscape General Medicine* 8, no. 3 (2006): 12.

2. Kevin Nugent and Wallace Smart, "Attention-Deficit/Hyperactivity Disorder in Postsecondary Students," *Neuropsychiatric Disease and Treatment* 10 (2014): 1781.

3. "Major and Career Search," The College Board, bigfuture.collegeboard.org/majors-careers. Accessed January 2, 2018.

4. Nugent and Smart, "Attention-Deficit/Hyperactivity Disorder in Postsecondary Students," 1781.

5. Tereza Killianova, "Risky Behavior," in *Encyclopedia of Behavioral Medicine*, ed. Marc D. Gellman and J. Rick Turner (Springer, 2013), link.springer.com/referenceworkentry/10.1007%2F978-1-4419-1005-9_1551. Accessed January 2, 2018.

6. R. G. Klein and J. Biederman, "ADHD Long-Term Outcomes: Comorbidity, Secondary Conditions, and Health Risk Behaviors," In *ADHD Workshop* (Atlanta, GA: Centers for Disease Control and Prevention, 1999), www.cdc.gov/ncbddd/adhd/workshops/outcomes.html. Accessed January 1, 2018.

7. Courtney Zulauf and Timothy E. Wilens, "ADHD, Cigarette Smoking, and Substance Abuse: An Intoxicating Combination," *Contemporary Pediatrics* 29, no. 11 (2012): 48–59.

8. "Fact Sheets—Binge Drinking," Centers for Disease Control and Prevention," www.cdc.gov/alcohol/fact-sheets/binge-drinking.htm. Accessed January 2, 2018.

9. Biederman and Faraone, "The Effects of Attention-Deficit/Hyperactivity Disorder on Employment," 12.

10. Ron de Graaf, Ronald C. Kessler, John Fayyad, Margaret ten Have, Jordi Alonso, Matthias Angermeyer, Guilherme Borges, et al. "The Prevalence and Effects of Adult Attention-Deficit/Hyperactivity Disorder (ADHD) on the Performance of Workers: Results from the WHO World Mental Health Survey Initiative," *Occupational and Environmental Medicine* 65, no. 12 (2008): 835–42, www.ncbi.nlm.nih.gov/pmc/articles/PMC2665789/. Accessed January 2, 2018.

11. Russell Barkley, "We're Hiring: ADHD-Friendly Careers," *ADDitude*, www.additudemag.com/adhd-friendly-jobs/. Accessed January 2, 2018.

12. Russell Barkley, "Fact Sheet: Attention Deficit Hyperactivity Disorder (ADHD) Topics," www.russellbarkley.org/factsheets/adhd-facts.pdf. Accessed January 2, 2018.

---

a. Anonymous student, "Words Just Came Out of My Mouth Before They Went through My Head," ADHD Awareness Month, October 3, 2014, www.adhdawarenessmonth.org/words-just-came-out-of-my-mouth-before-they-went-through-my-head/. Accessed January 15, 2018.

b. TEDx Talks, "Not Just LIVING but THRIVING with ADHD: Angela Aguirre: TEDxCal StateLA," YouTube video published June 8, 2017, www.youtube.com/watch?v=I0DLQ8 MUgTk. Accessed January 2, 2018.

Resources

1. "About," TED, www.ted.com/about/our-organization. Accessed January 3, 2018.
2. "CHADD Funding Sources," CHADD, www.chadd.org/About-CHADD/CHADD-Funding-Sources.aspx. Accessed January 15, 2018; Understood.org, www.understood.org/en. Accessed January 15, 2018; Attention Deficit Disorder Association, add.org/about-adda/. Accessed January 15, 2018.

a. ADHD Awareness Coalition, "October Is the ADHD Awareness Month," http://www.adh-dawarenessmonth.org/. Accessed January 15, 2018.

Resources

Having access to resources when you have ADHD is important. *Resources* is a broad term used to describe things that can help you. Some resources allow you to access the newest and most useful information. Some resources are people in the field of ADHD. Some resources can be other teens who deal with the day-to-day struggles of having ADHD. Technology is also a good resource that can help you gain information, connect with others, and help you with day-to-day tasks.

Types of Resources

Informational Resources

There are many places to get information on ADHD. Knowing why and what kind of information you need can help in picking the right resource. If you do a web search on ADHD, many links come up—some good, some not so good, some factual, and some people's opinions. Some are highly technical and meant for professionals, and some are written in a way that is easy to understand. How can you tell what resources you should listen to or read and which ones are not so great? This is a good question and one we will try to answer in this chapter.

Connecting with Others

Connecting with other people can be helpful if you have ADHD. There are lots of people who can be great resources: professionals who can give you treatment or information, people who have ADHD, friends of friends with ADHD who would like to help support or be part of a community of people who are affected by ADHD. These types of resources can be accessed through an online support group or by meeting with other people in person. By connecting with others you can find people who are going through the same experience and can give you a sense of community and belonging, as well as a place to talk.

Technological Resources

Technology can be used to help people with ADHD in a lot of different ways. For example, it can be used to help you access some of the informational resources that are listed in this chapter; it can make websites available through your computer or smartphone. Technology can also be used to help you gain access to some of the human resources that are listed in this chapter through web searches, videos, or other media. However, in addition to helping you gain access to other resources, technology can actually be its own resource. In the same way a calculator can help you do math, technologies, apps, and programs can help you organize yourself or cope with ADHD.

Questions to Ask Yourself

What type of resource do I need?

- Informational
- Human
- Technology

How will I access this resource?

- Through the Internet
- Through professionals
- Through reading materials

What kind of resource do I want?

- Highly technical language or easy to read
- Well-established facts or cutting-edge research
- Information about the law or education
- A way to connect with others
- Opinions or facts
- Help staying organized

Finally, when it comes to information, everyone has his or her own point of view. No source of information is ever completely right all of the time. When reading anything, you should ask yourself, where is this resource coming from? Is it an advertisement or the result of science? Who is paying for or funding this resource? For example, a study that states eating pickles reduces the risk of cancer may sound promising. You may even want to go out and buy a ten-pound jar of pickles. However, if the study was funded by the national pickle association and published in the international journal of pickles, you may want to think about where the information is coming from. Maybe eating all those pickles is no more healthy than eating an apple a day. However, the pickle people do not feel the need to tell you that extra piece of information. Maybe the person who is publishing the study has a lot to gain if people buy more pickles. Sometimes when you want to know the whole story, it is best to check more than one resource to see if it agrees or disagrees and why.

Different types of resources include the following:

- Government websites
- Professional organizations
- Nonprofit organizations
- Scientific literature
- TV and radio
- Podcasts
- YouTube
- Apps
- Social media
- The human connection
- Books

Government Websites

Generally speaking government websites are a good place to start for reliable information. Many government websites end in .gov. Government websites like the Individuals with Disabilities Education Act or the US Department of Education provide updated resources and information. Other government websites such as the Centers for Disease Control, National Institute of Health, or National Institute of Mental Health provide information on ADHD and health statistics for the United States. Government websites report information that was obtained through research that is high quality and has been subject to review by experts in the field. They are also a great resource to find out about the law. The info obtained from government websites can be dry and contain "just the facts." The statistics on government websites are good for school reports.

- Individuals with Disabilities Education Act: sites.ed.gov/idea/
- US Department of Education: www.ed.gov
- Centers for Disease Control: www.cdc.gov
- National Institute of Health: www.nih.gov
- National Institute of Mental Health: www.nimh.nih.gov

Many other resources use data that is obtained from these websites. If you want to hear what people are saying about ADHD, listen to people's opinions or find support, there are other places you can look.

Professional Organizations

Professional organizations are also a good place to find information about ADHD. Many of the professionals who work in the field of education and mental health belong to a professional organization. For example, many psychologists belong to the American Psychological Association, and physicians may belong to the American Medical Association. Professional organizations help to make rules for the best way to practice for professionals. They also produce research, distribute information, and more. Not all professional organizations are as well established or have as many members as others. Organizations such as the American Psychological Association and the American Medical Association are large, reputable, and well-established resources of information for ADHD, although there are many others as well. Most professional organizations can be viewed by checking their website. American Academy of Child and Adolescent Psychiatry contains a youth resource center.

- American Psychological Association: www.apa.org
- American Medical Association: www.ama-assn.org
- American Academy of Child and Adolescent Psychiatry: www.aacap.org
- National Association of School Psychologists: www.nasponline.org

Nonprofit/Organizations

Other organizations, such as Children and Adults with ADHD (CHADD), Understood.org, or the Attention Deficit Disorder Association are nonprofit. These are not considered professional organizations. The purpose of these groups is to provide information and connect people with similar interests and challenges and help people. Often, these organizations have highly respected professionals who sit on their advisory boards.

Nonprofit organizations are sometimes funded by government grants, private donations, and sales. The organizations listed here contain a wealth of useful information on ADHD. These groups provide scientific information in an easy-to-read format. Some of these organizations have thousands of members. They also contain opinions, online communities, and support. If you have specific questions about each organization, you can access its website directly and check it out.

Have you have ever watched a TED or a TEDx video? TED stands for Technology Education and Design. TED is an example of a nonprofit agency that is dedicated to spreading knowledge and "big ideas."[1] The TEDx program involves independently organized TED events. There are many TED and TEDx talks on ADHD. They can be accessed through the TED and TEDx websites.

Social media can be a great way to connect with others who are going through similar experiences. © *iStock / Halfpoint*

- Understood for learning and attention issues: www.understood.org
- Children and Adults with Attention-Deficit/Hyperactivity Disorder: www.chadd.org
- Attention Deficit Disorder Association: www.adda.org
- TED and TEDx talks: www.ted.com[2]

> **! Did You Know?**
>
> October is ADHD awareness month. Check out links for the ADHD awareness month 2017.[a]

Scientific Literature

Scientific literature is another way to find information about ADHD. Much of the literature is published in scientific journals. Reputable scientific journals have a very strict process in order to publish articles in them. Top professionals review all scientific articles before they can be published in journals to make sure they are accurate and of high quality. Examples are the *Journal of the American Medical Association* or *Nature*.

Scientific literature is often written for professionals or experts. It can be very hard to read and understand for people who are not professionals. Scientists often use highly technical language that can seem like a foreign language for those of us who are not scientists.

For this reason there is also popular scientific literature. Since not all of us are experts, the point of popular literature is to explain the findings of a scientific study. These could include magazines or online magazines that make highly scientific literature more understandable. They summarize the information for the reader. Many times the magazine or article will tell you what journal the information came from.

A word of caution: scientists can have very different opinions about the same topics. The scientific method that you learn in school teaches you to observe, make hypotheses, and test them to find out if they are true. Sometimes the results that different scientists come up with seem to prove the opposite thing. As the old expression goes, there are three sides to every story: your side, my side, and the truth, even if no one is lying. You may ask yourself, how can this happen? Well this is part of science. When this happens, the answer is to do some more experiments to find out why. For example, one scientist does an experiment and finds that kids with ADHD are better at cooking, but another scientist finds that kids with ADHD are not as good at cooking. A third scientist does an experiment to find out why scientists do not agree about how well kids with ADHD cook. This illustrates why it's wise not to take all of your information from one study or source; this probably isn't a great way to find out the real answer. Always look for multiple resources of information before you make your opinion.

TV and Radio

There are a lot of different types of information that you can get on TV or the radio including news about ADHD, talk shows that have ADHD topics, informative programming, entertainment, and more. Television and radio are a great way to get information as long as you know who your information is coming from and what the point of view is. Remember: TV and radio are usually paid for by advertising and also large companies and that information, including science, can have different points of view. This means that some people will only talk about the science that agrees with their own point of view. Make sure that you know the point of view of the show you are watching or listening to and what other sources think of that point of view.

Podcasts

Podcasts are a relatively new way of distributing information. They are episodes that can be in audio or video format on various topics. Podcasts are different from

Professionals in the Field of ADHD Who Have Made Podcasts

- Dr. Ned Hallowell: Distraction podcast
- *ADDitude* Magazine: ADHD expert podcasts

  ◦ Dr. Russell Barkley

  ◦ Dr. Thomas Brown

  ◦ Dr. Ned Hallowell

  ◦ Dr. Stephen Hinshaw

  ◦ Dr. Daniel Amen

the radio because you can download podcasts to your mobile device and listen to them. Podcasts are a convenient way to use technology to get info. Podcasts can be created by anyone and promote almost any view—positive, negative, true, or false. Be informed about whatever podcast you listen to. There are some highly respected professionals in the field that have podcasts related to ADHD.

These are great places to start when looking for information about ADHD. Podcasts are also very easy to listen to when you are walking, taking the bus, or making lunch. They do not require you to sit and read for hours and can be an easy way of learning without having to "study."

YouTube

YouTube can also be a great source of information on just about anything. Almost anyone can upload and watch anything on YouTube. Just as with other sources of information be aware of who is uploading what you are watching and make sure the information is accurate.

Apps

There are many different applications that run on smartphones and tablets that could be useful for individuals with ADHD. Some applications are specifically meant for people with ADHD, and some are just helpful in general. Some apps allow you to access information, and some apps can help you with planning and organizing. There are apps that help budget time, schedule, keep track of sleep, decrease procrastination, and even keep you on track and productive. The app for *ADDitude* magazine gives you one-click access to ADHD resources from your smartphone.

Driving apps can help you get from place to place in the quickest way possible. They can also let you know what the local speed limits are, how traffic will affect your trip, and re-route you when needed. Organizational applications can help you be on time, leave on time, or stay on task. People with ADHD have been known to have sleep disturbance. Maybe you need help waking up in the morning or going to sleep at night. Perhaps you are a "snoozer," hitting the snooze button many times, making you late; there are apps to help with that. Homework applications can help you organize your homework, meet deadlines, budget time, and break assignments into steps. Shopping and finance applications can help you budget and save money. There is an enormous number of apps that can help organize life's challenges and be useful for individuals with ADHD.

Social Media

Social media is a great way to instantly connect with others who are going through the same experiences as you. It can also be a good way to get up-to-the minute information. There are many groups on social media, including Twitter and Face-

TED has its own free app that you can download for your smartphone to listen to the talks.
© iStock / wutwhanfoto

book, that are specifically geared toward ADHD. Positive aspects of social media are that they can give one a sense of community and instant feedback. Social media can also provide ways to ask questions and get answers from others who are going through similar experiences.

Although there are many positives to social media, there are some things to watch out for as well. Social media groups can be started by almost anyone according to the rules of the social media site. It is important to understand that although there are people running the groups, most of their content is the opinion of those who are members. Some groups are open to anyone and some groups are closed to only certain people. This leaves room for negative people whose purpose on social media is to say negative things to others. It is also important to understand that anything that you post online can be distributed and shared with anyone on the Internet.

Online Campaigns

Through many social media outlets online campaigns sometimes pop up to bring awareness to an issue. Campaigns such as the ice bucket challenge were used to bring awareness to ALS (Lou Gehrig's) disease and research. There have been such campaigns for mental health as well and can usually be found by searching trending topics on the Internet.

The Human Connection

None of the resources that have been listed are "in person." Remember other people can be some of the best resources out there. If you are in high school or college, many schools have campus or school organizations. They are a great way to connect with others who have the same interests or hobbies as you and may lead to making friends as well.

In addition, mental health professionals are a great resource and are often accessible in schools (read chapter 7 for treatment options). Many schools have school psychologists, mental health counselors, guidance counselors, or social workers. These people can provide you with guidance if you are having a hard time or need someone to talk to. Many colleges have mental health clinics that are paid for by the school's tuition.

Some organizations such as CHADD or Understood.org also provide advocacy about the topic of ADHD. Volunteering with advocacy groups can be a great way for you to help the cause by getting out accurate information about ADHD and ways to help others. These include:

- Support groups
- Student disability office

- Counselors, school psychologists or social workers, or other mental health professionals
- Advocacy groups

Books

Books are another way to get information about ADHD. There are many great books that are written for teens and adults. It is important to understand that books can be written by anyone and can represent anyone's opinion about a topic, even this book that you are reading right now. One may publish a book with one point of view and someone else may publish with another. Either may be right or wrong or neither. Books that are written by well-established and well-known scientists or doctors or authors are a good place to start. Sometimes scientists or professionals will summarize their scientific literature, making it easier to read and understand. Examples of well-known authors of books on ADHD are.

- Dr. Ned Hallowell
- Dr. Russell Barkley
- Dr. Thomas Brown

Some books are meant to describe the experience of the author. Many people with ADHD have published books about their own experiences. These books may contain scientific facts but that is not their main purpose. They are books that are meant to help others or explain a person's experience with ADHD. Books by authors with ADHD are a great resource to understand the experience and normalize the struggles and successes that people with ADHD go through in life.

Additional Resources for ADHD Information:

ADDitude magazine—Accessible through the *ADDitude* website, this magazine has lots of different articles on all different aspects of ADHD. www.additudemag.com.

Attention Magazine—Published by CHADD, this magazine or articles from it can be downloaded from CHADD's website. www.chadd.org.

LD online—This website provides resources for ADHD and other learning disabilities. ldonline.org.

TotallyADD.com—This website was created by an actor, comedy writer, and comedian and has lots of interviews and information relating to ADHD. totallyadd.com/.

Understood—This website has lots of information on ADHD and other learning disabilities. www.understood.org.

Index

About the Author

John Aspromonte, PsyD, is a school psychologist working in special education, including students with ADHD. He holds a doctorate in psychology from Fairleigh Dickinson University, a master's degree in school psychology from Fordham University, and master's degrees in neuroscience and education from Columbia University. In the last fifteen years he has been working in the fields of neuroscience, mental health, and education. Dr. Aspromonte lives in New Jersey with his wife and son.